VOLUME 11

NEW TESTAMENT

THE NEW COLLEGEVILLE BIBLE COMMENTARY

THE LETTER TO THE HEBREWS

Daniel J. Harrington, S.J.

D0829811

SERIES EDITOR

Daniel Durken, O.S.B.

LITURGICAL PRESS

Collegeville, Minnesota

www.litpress.org

Nihil obstat: Robert C. Harren, *Censor deputatus.*
Imprimatur: ✠ John F. Kinney, Bishop of St. Cloud, Minnesota, December 29, 2005.

Design by Ann Blattner.

	3	4	5	6	7	8	9

Library of Congress Cataloging-in-Publication Data

Harrington, Daniel J.
    The letter to the Hebrews / Daniel J. Harrington.
       p. cm. — (The new Collegeville Bible commentary. New Testament ; v. 11)
    Summary: "Complete biblical texts with sound, scholarly based commentary that is written at a pastoral level; the Scripture translation is that of the New American Bible with Revised New Testament and Revised Psalms (1991)" —Provided by publisher.
    Includes bibliographical references.
    ISBN-13: 978-0-8146-2870-6 (pbk. : alk. paper)
    ISBN-10: 0-8146-2870-2 (pbk. : alk. paper)
    1. Bible. N.T. Hebrews—Commentaries. I. Title. II. Series.
BS2775.53.H37   2005
227'.87077—dc22

                                                            2005017935

CONTENTS

ABBREVIATIONS

Books of the Bible

Acts—Acts of the Apostles
Amos—Amos
Bar—Baruch
1 Chr—1 Chronicles
2 Chr—2 Chronicles
Col—Colossians
1 Cor—1 Corinthians
2 Cor—2 Corinthians
Dan—Daniel
Deut—Deuteronomy
Eccl (or Qoh)—Ecclesiastes
Eph—Ephesians
Esth—Esther
Exod—Exodus
Ezek—Ezekiel
Ezra—Ezra
Gal—Galatians
Gen—Genesis
Hab—Habakkuk
Hag—Haggai
Heb—Hebrews
Hos—Hosea
Isa—Isaiah
Jas—James
Jdt—Judith
Jer—Jeremiah
Job—Job
Joel—Joel
John—John
1 John—1 John
2 John—2 John
3 John—3 John
Jonah—Jonah
Josh—Joshua
Jude—Jude
Judg—Judges
1 Kgs—1 Kings
2 Kgs—2 Kings

Lam—Lamentations
Lev—Leviticus
Luke—Luke
1 Macc—1 Maccabees
2 Macc—2 Maccabees
Mal—Malachi
Mark—Mark
Matt—Matthew
Mic—Micah
Nah—Nahum
Neh—Nehemiah
Num—Numbers
Obad—Obadiah
1 Pet—1 Peter
2 Pet—2 Peter
Phil—Philippians
Phlm—Philemon
Prov—Proverbs
Ps(s)—Psalms
Rev—Revelation
Rom—Romans
Ruth—Ruth
1 Sam—1 Samuel
2 Sam—2 Samuel
Sir—Sirach
Song—Song of Songs
1 Thess—1 Thessalonians
2 Thess—2 Thessalonians
1 Tim—1 Timothy
2 Tim—2 Timothy
Titus—Titus
Tob—Tobit
Wis—Wisdom
Zech—Zechariah
Zeph—Zephaniah

The Letter to the Hebrews

Among the books of the New Testament, the Letter to the Hebrews stands out for its rhetorical and theological brilliance. It is arguably the greatest Christian sermon ever preached or written. Its author deserves to be revered as the patron saint of preachers. He has presented the essential claim of Christian faith that Christ died for our sins in a persuasive argument with a deep emotional appeal. One way to introduce this book is to describe Hebrews as a sermon in written form, of uncertain origin, intended to encourage perseverance in Christian faith.

A sermon in written form

The author describes his work as a "message of encouragement" (13:22), which most interpreters take to mean a speech or sermon in written form. The only literary features that might qualify Hebrews as a letter or epistle are the travel plans and personal greetings that appear in 13:23-24. These features may have been attached to the sermon as it was sent from one community to another. Or perhaps they were interpolated into the text to promote its association with the corpus of Pauline letters.

Hebrews is no ordinary sermon. Indeed, it is a highly literary and rhetorical sermon that is at once simple and subtle. The basic theological point is simple: Christ is both the perfect sacrifice for sins and the priest who offers himself as a sacrifice. The work's sophisticated use of the Greek language indicates a high level of education on the author's part. As a good preacher, the author interweaves expositions of biblical texts and exhortations to faith and good actions. While he sometimes appears to make a formal delineation between exposition and exhortation, he always joins the two. Exposition leads into exhortation, and exhortation leads to further exposition. He announces his main themes beforehand, repeats keywords, begins and ends units in similar ways (a technique called inclusion), and uses various rhetorical devices (alliteration, arguments "from the lesser to the greater," etc.).

The rhetorical handbooks of the Greco-Roman world distinguished three kinds of speeches: forensic or judicial (used in accusing or defending someone in a legal trial), deliberative (used in persuading a public assembly to take action), and epideictic (used at public memorial occasions to confirm a community's values by praise or blame).

Hebrews best fits the conventions of epideictic rhetoric. It celebrates the greatness of Jesus as the Son of God and as the great high priest and promotes the values that he stood for. It offers comparisons with the angels, Moses, the priests of the old covenant, and Melchizedek to extol the greatness of Jesus. It praises and blames those who are being addressed and seeks to confirm their positive beliefs in the hope of rousing them from spiritual sluggishness and of rescuing them from the danger of falling away from the Christian faith.

The basic outline of Hebrews is clear enough. The first main part (1:1–4:13) establishes Jesus' superiority as God's Son to the angels and to Moses and uses various biblical texts to explore Jesus' significance and the need for persevering in Christian life. The second main part (4:14–10:18) concerns the high priesthood of Christ and the perfect sacrifice of Christ. The third main part (10:19–13:25) reflects on the nature of Christian life and the need for perseverance and endurance in the face of suffering. There are many much more elaborate outlines. But even the simple tripartite outline is not entirely adequate, since the author is so skilled in making transitions, in anticipating themes to be developed later, and in integrating biblical expositions and exhortations.

Of uncertain origin

The authorship of Hebrews has always been controversial. The early church writer Origen said: "But who wrote the epistle, in truth God knows" (Eusebius, *Ecclesiastical History* 6.25.14). Although the reference to "our brother Timothy" in 13:23 might suggest Pauline authorship, the language, literary style and form, and theology are very different from those of Paul's genuine letters. The attributions to Barnabas (see Acts 4:36) and Apollos (see Acts 18:24) are at best guesses.

The sermon in written form is anonymous. The author never names himself, nor does he reveal much personal information. But some reliable statements can be made about his identity. The author had sophisticated knowledge of the Old Testament in its Greek translation and displays a good familiarity with the techniques of Jewish biblical interpretation. He must have been Jewish. Nevertheless, he was convinced that God had done something so dramatically new and significant through the life, death, resurrection, and exaltation of Jesus that the institutions of the old covenant with Israel through Moses on Mount Sinai were no longer effective. They were only types or shadows of the realities fulfilled in Christ. As he addresses his audience, the author seeks to serve as their teacher and pastoral guide. To respect the mixed genre of Hebrews as a sermon in written form, I refer in the commentary to the author, the writer, and the preacher alternatively, as well as to the readers, the congregation, the community, and the audience.

Those originally addressed in Hebrews seem to have been Jewish Christians who had embraced Christianity with enthusiasm but were wavering and in danger of giving into discouragement and falling away, especially in the face of suffering (see 12:3-11). It is very tempting to locate the community in Rome on the basis of 13:24 ("those from Italy send you greetings") and the earliest attestations of Hebrews in Clement of Rome's first letter to the Corinthians (1 Clement). But there is no certainty here. Neither is the date of composition certain, since practically anytime between A.D. 50 and 100 is possible. The absence of any reference to the destruction of the Jerusalem temple in A.D. 70 might suggest an early date (the fifties or sixties), though one must admit that the author is more interested in explaining Scripture than in commenting on contemporary events. With these cautions in mind, the hypothesis that Hebrews was addressed to a Jewish Christian community at Rome in the late fifties or early sixties of the first century A.D. remains nonetheless the most attractive setting.

Uncertainty also surrounds the history-of-religions background of Hebrews, so much so that this issue is often called "the mystery of Hebrews." Although some of the author's biblical expositions sound something like what one finds in the writings of Philo of Alexandria, he seems more interested in typology than in allegory. The portrayal of Melchizedek as a heavenly figure in some Dead Sea Scrolls was initially thought to illumine Hebrews 7. But it now appears that the author simply gives his own christological readings of the pertinent biblical texts. Concepts that developed in Gnosticism are sometimes read back into Hebrews, but again the results only highlight the author's theological originality. The New Testament document that is closest to Hebrews is 1 Peter. It is a sermon addressed to alienated and suffering Christians, who are urged to find encouragement and hope in the example of Christ the Suffering Servant. While those addressed in 1 Peter were mainly Gentile Christians, the main audience for Hebrews appears to have been Jewish Christians.

To encourage perseverance

Hebrews is a sustained theological reflection on the very early Christian confession of faith that Christ died for us and for our sins. This confession appears both in Paul's writings (see Gal 1:4; 3:13; 2 Cor 5:14, 21; Rom 5:6; 14:15) and in the pre-Pauline creedal formulas that Paul quotes (see 1 Cor 11:24; 15:3; Rom 3:25-26).

The author of Hebrews shares and develops the idea of the sacrificial nature of Christ's death and its atoning value. However, his most distinctive theological contribution is the concept of the high priesthood of Christ. According to early Christian tradition (see Mark 10:45; 14:24; and especially 14:36), Jesus willingly offered himself in death. Since the one who offers a sacrifice is a priest, the author endeavors to show that Christ can be called a priest despite the fact that he was not born into the Jewish priestly tribe of Levi. The basic theological claim of Hebrews is that Christ is both the perfect sacrifice for sins and the priest who offered himself as that sacrifice.

In developing this thesis, the author assumes that Christ is the key to the Old Testament Scriptures. Not content to leave behind the Old Testament, he argues that the words of Scripture only make sense when attributed to Christ or applied to him. His favorite texts are the messianic Psalms 2 and 110, and in his exhortations he calls upon Psalms 8 and 95 among others. The description of the Day of Atonement ritual in Leviticus 16 is the basic source for establishing Christ's sacrifice and priesthood.

The author insists on the superiority of Christ as the Son of God over the angels and over Moses. Because Christ is both the high priest and the perfect sacrifice, his saving action—his death, resurrection, and exaltation taken as a single event—has made possible the forgiveness of sins, confident access to God, and hope for eternal life with God.

The people addressed in Hebrews seem to be having a hard time in accepting the absolute sufficiency of Christ's perfect sacrifice on the cross. If they are to persevere in Christian faith, they need a spiritual renewal. At various points the author addresses their situation directly with stern warnings and words of encouragement. Most of all, he hopes that his biblical-theological presentation of Christ's sacrifice and priesthood will give them the appropriate theological framework to put aside their doubts and spiritual sluggishness and to revitalize their Christian faith and practice.

To that end the author portrays Christ as the pioneer (the one who has already gone before us) and the leader for those who follow him on the way to eternal life with God. The risen and exalted Christ remains a mediator on our behalf in the present (9:24) and will appear again to bring salvation in the future (9:28). His perfect sacrifice renders unnecessary the sacrifices and priests of the old covenant. In fact, these persons and institutions were at best types or signs that have received their full definition in Christ.

Two hard questions

Does Hebrews illumine the Christian priesthood? The work is mainly concerned with the priesthood of the Old Testament and the priesthood of

Christ. It does not speak directly about the communal priesthood of all Christians (see 1 Pet 2:9; Rev 1:6; 5:10; 20:6) or about the Christian ministerial priesthood. However, many Christians have found in Christ's priesthood an apt metaphor for describing Christian life in general. It has also been traditional among Catholics and other Christians to find in Christ's priesthood the model and dynamism for the ministerial priesthood. But some Protestants regard Christ's priesthood to be the end of all claims to priesthood, since his perfect "once for all" sacrifice has rendered unnecessary all other sacrifices and priesthoods. The problem is that Hebrews is silent on this important question and can be (and has been) read as supporting or denying all the various positions about priesthood.

Is Hebrews anti-Jewish? Since both the author and his audience seem to have been Jews, such a charge seems unfair and anachronistic. In fact, Hebrews is an interpretation of Judaism in the light of Christ. Without the authoritative Scriptures of Israel and the great heroes and institutions of the biblical tradition, there would be little substance to Hebrews. And yet perhaps more than any other New Testament writer, the author of Hebrews insists that the old covenant, priesthood, and sacrificial system have been superseded through Christ. Modern Christian readers need to respect the historical (Jewish) setting of Hebrews and to be sensitive to the anti-Jewish potential of the text when it is taken out of its first-century Jewish Christian context.

Reading Hebrews

Hebrews is a sermon in written form. It presents a sustained theological argument, and so it may be helpful to read it straight through at one sitting. Its rhetoric and theology are highly sophisticated and difficult for modern readers, and therefore it deserves careful study, with the commentary that follows as a guide. It may be helpful to look up the Old Testament texts that the author quotes in order to appreciate how he handles these texts from his christological perspective. One must be aware, however, that the author used the ancient Greek version (Septuagint) of the Old Testament, which often differs from the Hebrew text on which our modern translations are based. A communal reading of this sermon in written form might serve as a final exercise. A well-prepared and reverent group reading of the whole text takes about fifty minutes. The exercise will help those who have worked through this difficult text to appreciate better the truth of the author's own comment: "The word of God is living and effective, sharper than any two-edged sword" (4:12).

The Letter to the Hebrews

I. Introduction

◁ 1 ¹In times past, God spoke in partial and various ways to our ancestors through the prophets; ²in these last days, he spoke to us through a son, whom he made heir of all things and through whom he created the universe,

◁ ³who is the refulgence of his glory,
the very imprint of his being,

and who sustains all things by his
mighty word.
When he had accomplished purification from sins,
he took his seat at the right hand of
the Majesty on high,
⁴as far superior to the angels
as the name he has inherited is
more excellent than theirs.

GOD'S SON AND GOD'S WORD

Heb 1:1–4:13

1:1-4 Prologue: Jesus as the climax of divine revelation

The prologue serves as an introduction or overture to the entire sermon by calling attention to major themes and to the pivotal place of Jesus in the history of salvation. Using the device of alliteration, in which several words begin with the same letter ("past . . . partial . . . prophets"), the author begins in 1:1-2a by showing how Jesus continues the story of God's communication to Israel and brings it to a definitive point or climax. He develops the idea by four contrasts. (1) Whereas God spoke "in times past," now he has spoken "in these last days" (the new era ushered in by Jesus and issuing in the fullness of God's kingdom). (2) Whereas God spoke "to our ancestors" (historic Israel), now he has spoken "to us" (the Christian community). (3) Whereas God spoke "through the prophets" (including Moses, Joshua, and David, as well as those known traditionally as the prophets), now he has spoken through "a son" (Jesus).

▶ This symbol indicates a cross reference number in the *Catechism of the Catholic Church*. See page 63 for number citations.

11

A view of the Dome of the Rock from the Mount of Olives

II. The Son Higher than the Angels

Messianic Enthronement. [5]For to which of the angels did God ever say:

> "You are my son; this day I have
> begotten you"?

Or again:

> "I will be a father to him, and he
> shall be a son to me"?

[6]And again, when he leads the firstborn into the world, he says:

> "Let all the angels of God worship
> him."

[7]Of the angels he says:

> "He makes his angels winds
> and his ministers a fiery flame";

[8]but of the Son:

---

(4) Whereas God spoke "in partial and various ways," now he has spoken in a full and definitive way (through Jesus).

In describing the person and work of Jesus in 1:2b-3, the author highlights his identity as the Messiah and as Wisdom. Jesus' identity as the Messiah is developed with the help of two psalms (2 and 110) that serve as major texts throughout the sermon. Both psalms originated in the ritual associated with the coronation of kings in ancient Israel. The king was "anointed" as part of his coronation, and the word "Messiah" means "the anointed one." By declaring Jesus as "heir of all things" (see Ps 2:8) and as taking his seat at God's right hand (Ps 110:1), the author tells us right away that Jesus is the Messiah of Jewish expectations. What historic Israel hoped from its kings, Jesus has provided.

Jesus' identity as the Wisdom of God is established by evoking terms and motifs from various Old Testament passages in which Wisdom is portrayed as the agent of God in creation (see Proverbs 8, Sirach 24, and Wisdom 7). The author affirms that Jesus was God's agent in creating the universe ("through whom he created the universe," see Prov 8:30; Wis 7:22), that he reflects God's glory and represents God's being (see Wis 7:26), and that he carries on God's work of creation ("who sustains all things"). The motif of Jesus as the Wisdom of God is prominent in early Christian hymns preserved in other New Testament books, most notably Colossians 1:15-20 and John 1:1-18.

While identifying Jesus as God's Messiah and Wisdom, the author also introduces his major theme of Jesus' role in the "purification from sins," a work accomplished through his sacrificial death on the cross and his subsequent exaltation to the heavenly throne of God. Likewise, in 1:4 he announces the theme that will be developed in what follows immediately: the superiority of Jesus to the angels. This theme is related to the superior "name" that Jesus bears as the Son of God. The author's task will be to show why the Son should be regarded as superior to the angels.

"Your throne, O God, stands forever
and ever;
and a righteous scepter is the
scepter of your kingdom.
⁹You loved justice and hated wicked-
ness;
therefore God, your God,
anointed you
with the oil of gladness above
your companions";

¹⁰and:

"At the beginning, O Lord, you
established the earth,
and the heavens are the works
of your hands.

¹¹They will perish, but you remain;
and they will all grow old like a
garment.
¹²You will roll them up like a cloak,
and like a garment they will be
changed.
But you are the same, and your
years will have no end."
¹³But to which of the angels has he ever ▷
said:
"Sit at my right hand
until I make your enemies your
footstool"?
¹⁴Are they not all ministering spirits sent ▷
to serve, for the sake of those who are
to inherit salvation?

1:5-14 Jesus as superior to the angels

Why the author felt compelled to take on this task is not certain. There is some evidence in the Dead Sea Scrolls and other early Jewish texts for veneration of angels. And some early Christians may have regarded Jesus as an angel. Or the issue may have been entirely theoretical.

The device that the author uses to establish Jesus' superiority to the angels is a chain (or *catena*) of biblical quotations. While the *catena* genre was used by Jewish writers of the times, the author of Hebrews makes it serve his christological purpose. For him, Christ is the key to the Scriptures, and so all the biblical texts that he quotes are assumed to speak to or about Christ. There are three pairs of quotations (1:5, 6-7, 8-12), along with a single quotation of Psalm 110 (109):1 (1:13).

The introduction to the *catena* in 1:5a ("to which of the angels did God ever say") establishes that the purpose is to prove the superiority of the Son. The concluding comment in 1:14 about the angels as servants is a case of "inclusion," in which an argument is begun and ended in similar ways.

In 1:5 the first pair of quotations—Psalm 2:7 and 2 Samuel 7:14—serve to identify Jesus as God's Son and Messiah: "You are my son . . . he shall be a son to me." The assumption is that God is the speaker and addresses Jesus as his Messiah/Son. Part of the ideology of kingship in ancient Israel was that the king became God's "son" at his accession to the throne. And so when applied to Jesus, the terms "Messiah" and "Son" are synonyms.

In 1:6-7 the second pair of quotations—Deuteronomy 32:43/Psalm 97(96):7 and Psalm 104 (103):4—establish the inferiority of the angels to the

2 Exhortation to Faithfulness.

¹Therefore, we must attend all the more to what we have heard, so that we may not be carried away. ²For if the word announced through angels proved firm, and every transgression and disobedience received its just recompense, ³how shall we escape if we ignore so great a salvation? Announced originally through the Lord, it was confirmed for us by those who had heard. ⁴God added his testimony by signs, wonders, various acts of power, and distribution of the gifts of the holy Spirit according to his will.

Exaltation through Abasement. ⁵For it was not to angels that he subjected the world to come, of which we are speaking. ⁶Instead, someone has testified somewhere:

Son of God. The assumption is that God spoke these words when Jesus the Wisdom of God took on human flesh ("when he leads the first-born into the world") and that these words concern the Son of God. The first text says that the role of the angels is to worship the Son, and the second text presents the angels as instruments of God ("winds . . . a fiery flame").

In 1:8-12 the third pair of quotations—Psalm 45(44):7-8 and Psalm 102 (101):26-28—takes texts originally addressed to God and applies them to the Messiah/Son ("your throne, O God . . . O Lord, you established"). The emphasis is on the eternity of Jesus' reign as God's Messiah/Son ("forever and ever . . . God, your God, anointed you . . . your years will have no end"). While such things cannot be said of angels, applying these biblical affirmations about God to Christ suggests his own authority, eternity, and even divinity.

In 1:13 the final (single) quotation—Psalm 110(109):1—applies what was said by God to the king at his coronation ("sit at my right hand / until I make your enemies your footstool") to the resurrected and exalted Messiah/Son. Throughout Hebrews, the center of attention will be Jesus' death, resurrection, and exaltation understood as one great event. The *catena* concludes in 1:14 with a comment about the role of the angels as servants of God ("ministering spirits") on behalf of all those who seek salvation.

2:1-4 A call to commitment and responsibility

At many points in his sermon the author addresses his audience directly and challenges them to apply his message about Christ to their own situation. Even in his exhortations, however, he injects new theological considerations based on the Old Testament and on God's saving activity in Jesus.

As a good preacher, the author moves in 2:1 from the *catena* of biblical quotations to their significance for Christian life and includes himself

"What is man that you are mindful
of him,

or the son of man that you care
for him?

⁷You made him for a little while
lower than the angels;

you crowned him with glory
and honor,

⁸subjecting all things under his
feet."

In "subjecting" all things [to him], he left nothing not "subject to him." Yet at present we do not see "all things subject to him," ⁹but we do see Jesus "crowned with glory and honor" because he suffered death, he who "for a little while"

---

among those being addressed ("therefore we must attend . . ."). The expression "what we have heard" may refer to the gospel message in general, to the biblical passages applied to Christ in 1:5-14, or to Jesus as the Word of God—or all three at once. The danger that the audience faces is expressed by the phrase "so that we may not be carried away," which evokes the image of a ship failing to reach its harbor safely. The author fears that his people may drift away from the gospel that they had once embraced.

The warning in 2:2-3a builds on the case developed about the Son's superiority to the angels. It employs the rhetorical device of arguing "from the lesser to the greater" and assumes that the law was given to Moses on Sinai through the mediation of angels (see Acts 7:53; Gal 3:19). If the Mosaic Law given through angels punishes each and every transgression, how much more will God punish neglect of the salvation given through Christ. The logic is that the greater revelation (the gospel) given through the greater revealer (Christ) will exact greater punishment from those who fail to attend to it.

Having raised the threat of severe punishment, the author in 2:3b-4 reminds his audience about the nature of the salvation brought by Christ. It was announced by Jesus ("the Lord") and confirmed by the apostolic witnesses and by God through miracles ("signs, wonders, various acts of power") and through the gifts of the holy Spirit (not a major figure in Hebrews). Note the "trinitarian" dimension that serves as the framework for describing the saving work of Christ.

2:5-9 Jesus as the Son of Man

Having reflected on the significance of the salvation brought by Jesus for the community of faith, the author takes up again the theme of Jesus' superiority to the angels. According to a biblical tradition (see Deut 32:8; Dan 10:20-21; 12:1), God placed the world in the present age under the governance of angels. According to early Christian faith, however, the was made "lower than the angels," that by the grace of God he might taste death for everyone.

¹⁰For it was fitting that he, for whom and through whom all things exist, in bringing many children to glory, should make the leader to their salvation perfect through suffering. ¹¹He who consecrates and those who are being consecrated all have one origin. Therefore, he is not ashamed to call them "brothers," ¹²saying:

"I will proclaim your name to my brothers,
in the midst of the assembly I will praise you";

¹³and again:

"I will put my trust in him";

new age or "world to come" (2:5) has already been inaugurated in and through Christ. But the quotation of Psalm 110(109):1 in Hebrews 1:13 ("until I make your enemies your footstool") could give the impression that Christ's reign was still future. And so the author contends that Christ's reign is both present and future and that it began with Jesus' incarnation, death, and exaltation.

The biblical vehicle for the author's argument is Psalm 8:5-7(4-6), which is part of a meditation on the great dignity of human beings. The psalmist ("someone . . . somewhere") praises God ("you") for God's care and love for humankind ("man . . . the son of man") and observes that God has placed human beings a little lower than the angels and given them stewardship over the world (see Gen 1:26, 28).

True to his interpretive principle that Christ is the key to the Scriptures, the author assumes that Psalm 8 speaks about Christ as the "son of man." In his interpretation (2:8b-9), he affirms that God has already placed all creation under the governance of Christ as the Son of Man. The problem is that humans do not yet perceive Christ's sovereignty, though they surely will do so in the fullness of God's kingdom. What is now perceived through faith is the risen and exalted Christ ("crowned . . . with glory and honor"). His glorification followed from his suffering and death, when he was lower than the angels "for a little while" (the adverb is interpreted chronologically rather than qualitatively). The paradox is that Christ's humiliation in his passion became the occasion for the exaltation of us all. The idea that Christ's death was the perfect sacrifice for sins and opened up the possibility for the salvation of all humans is introduced by the concluding clause: "that by the grace of God he might taste death for everyone" (2:9).

2:10-18 Christ in solidarity with humans

The fundamental affirmation of Hebrews is expressed in 2:10: God ("for whom and through whom all things exist") made Jesus the pioneer

and again:

> "Behold, I and the children God has given me."

[14]Now since the children share in blood and flesh, he likewise shared in them, that through death he might destroy the one who has the power of death, that is, the devil, [15]and free those who through fear of death had been subject to slavery all their life. [16]Surely he did not help angels but rather the descendants of Abraham; [17]therefore, he had to become like his brothers in every way, that he might be a merciful and faithful high priest before God to expiate the sins of the people. [18]Because he

or champion ("leader") to bring all humans to salvation, and the way by which this goal was achieved was through the cross, in which Christ was made "perfect through suffering." This statement captures the self-sacrifice involved in Jesus' death on the cross as well as the atoning value of his death for others. Thus Jesus can be understood (as we will see) as both the priest (because he offered himself willingly) and the sacrifice (because his death was for us and for our sins).

Jesus' solidarity with humans and his special relationship with God are established in 2:11-13 by a series of Old Testament quotations. Both Christ ("he who consecrates") and humans ("those who are being consecrated") share a common origin in God and in humanity. And so Christ can call other humans "brothers." The first biblical quotation is Psalm 22:22(23)—from the prayer of the righteous sufferer, which is also the source of Jesus' last words on the cross, according to Mark (15:34) and Matthew (27:46). In the author's christological framework, Jesus ("I") confesses and praises God ("you") among his fellow humans ("to my brothers"). In the second biblical quotation (Isa 8:17-18), Christ ("I") professes trust in God ("in him") and identifies himself with other humans ("I and the children God has given me"). Thus Christ is the link or mediator between God and humans.

The classic question, Why did Christ become human? is taken up in 2:14-18. By sharing our humanity, Christ was able to render inoperative the devil as the one who has power over death and to free us from the fear of death that makes us slaves (2:14-15). The object of Christ's saving work was the "descendants of Abraham," which includes not only Israel as the chosen people of God but also the many nations of which Abraham was the father (2:16). Only by being fully human could Christ be both our priest ("a merciful and faithful high priest") and our sacrifice ("to expiate the sins of the people"). Only by being tested through suffering could Christ help us as we are being tested. These ideas about the priesthood of Christ will be developed at great length in chapters 5–10.

himself was tested through what he suffered, he is able to help those who are being tested.

III. Jesus, Faithful and Compassionate High Priest

3 Jesus, Superior to Moses. ¹Therefore, holy "brothers," sharing in a heavenly calling, reflect on Jesus, the apostle and high priest of our confession, ²who was faithful to the one who appointed him, just as Moses was "faithful in [all] his house." ³But he is worthy of more "glory" than Moses, as the founder of a house has more "honor" than the house itself. ⁴Every house is founded by someone, but the founder of all is God. ⁵Moses was "faithful in all his house" as a "servant" to testify to what would be spoken, ⁶but Christ was faithful as a son placed over his house. We are his house, if

---

3:1-6 Jesus as superior to Moses

The preacher returns in 3:1 to direct address. He reminds his congregation that as "brothers" of Christ and of one another, they share in the holiness that reflects God the holy one par excellence and in the call to eternal life with God. Identifying Jesus as "the apostle" (the one "sent" from God—the only New Testament application of this title to Christ) and "high priest" (a title already introduced in 2:17 and soon to become the center of attention), the author in 3:2 focuses on Jesus' fidelity to God as "the one who appointed him." He also introduces the figure of Moses and the characterization of Moses as "faithful in all his house."

This description of Moses comes from Numbers 12:7(8): "Not so with my servant Moses! / Throughout my house he bears my trust." In the Old Testament context, Moses appears as the instrument of God's revelation who is superior to Aaron, Miriam, and all other recipients of divine revelation. The "house" is Israel as the people of God, where Moses functioned as the "servant" of God.

In comparing Moses and Christ in 3:3-6, the author is more concerned to praise Christ than to denigrate Moses. He proceeds on two fronts: the house (3:3-4) and the servant (3:5-6). Just as the architect-builder of a house deserves more praise than the house itself, so God (and Christ as God's agent) deserves more praise than Moses in founding the people of God. Just as in a large household a son is more important than a servant, so Christ the Son is more important than Moses the servant in the people of God. Whereas Moses was a servant "in" God's house, Christ was a son placed "over" the house. Thus Jesus' faithfulness as God's Son was superior to the faithfulness of God's servant Moses.

The preacher concludes in 3:6b by identifying the Christian community as the "house" or people of God ("we are his house") and by warning

[only] we hold fast to our confidence and pride in our hope.

Israel's Infidelity a Warning.

◄ ⁷Therefore, as the holy Spirit says:
"Oh, that today you would hear his
voice,
⁸'Harden not your hearts as at
the rebellion
in the day of testing in the
desert,
⁹where your ancestors tested
and tried me
and saw my works ¹⁰for forty
years.
Because of this I was provoked
with that generation
and I said, 'They have always been of erring
heart,
and they do not know my
ways."
¹¹As I swore in my wrath,
"They shall not enter into my
rest." ' "

¹²Take care, brothers, that none of you may have an evil and unfaithful heart, so as to forsake the living God. ¹³En-courage yourselves daily while it is still "today," so that none of you may grow hardened by the deceit of sin. ¹⁴We have become partners of Christ if only we hold the beginning of the reality firm until the end, ¹⁵for it is said:

"Oh, that today you would hear his
voice:
'Harden not your hearts as at the
rebellion.' "

the community to retain their confidence and pride in what God has done and continues to do for them through Christ the Son. Otherwise they may cease to be God's house.

3:7-19 The negative example of Israel in the wilderness

A good preacher frequently offers a congregation positive examples to be imitated and negative examples to be avoided. As a way of challenging the congregation to emulate the fidelity displayed by Christ, the author presents the negative example of ancient Israel wandering in the wilder-ness between the exodus from Egypt to the entrance into the land of Canaan.

The main biblical text is Psalm 95(94):7b-11 (which is read in light of Numbers 14). The text is introduced as having logical significance ("there-fore") and as being from God ("as the holy Spirit says"). In Psalm 95 the admonition to be faithful follows an invitation to worship God, most ob-viously at the Jerusalem temple (Ps 95:1-7a). The admonition itself recalls the episode of Israel's rebellion in the wilderness (see Exod 17:1-17; Num 14:21-23). The place in which the rebellion took place was called in He-brew "Massah" (meaning "testing") and "Meribah" (meaning "quarrel-ing"). The text begins with a call to hear God's voice "today" (Heb 3:7b = Ps 95:7b). Then there is a warning to avoid the rebelliousness displayed by the Exodus generation in the wilderness for forty years (Heb 3:8-9 =

¹⁶Who were those who rebelled when they heard? Was it not all those who came out of Egypt under Moses? ¹⁷With whom was he "provoked for forty years"? Was it not those who had sinned, whose corpses fell in the desert? ¹⁸And to whom did he "swear that they should not enter into his rest,"

Ps 95:8-9). Finally,God recalls his anger at that generation and his resolve that they would not find "rest" in the land of Canaan (Heb 3:10-11 = Ps 95:10-11).

Having quoted this biblical text at length, the author in 3:12-15 makes an application to the situation of his audience in the first century A.D. First, in 3:12 he warns them against falling away from the living God, as the Exodus generation did, through "an evil and unfaithful heart." Then, in 3:13 he encourages them to regard every day as "today" and not to allow their hearts to be hardened. Finally, in 3:14-15 he warns them again that their partnership with Christ depends on remaining faithful "until the end." The final warning and the application in general are underscored by a repetition of Psalm 95:7b-8 and by bringing back the key words ("today . . . hear his voice . . . harden not your hearts . . . rebellion").

The application is an example of the actualization of Scripture. Just as the psalmist used the negative example of the Exodus generation to motivate people in his own generation, so the author of Hebrews applies both the example and the biblical text to early Christians in his own day. This process of actualization is carried on whenever the letter to the Hebrews is proclaimed today, since "the word of God is living and effective" (4:12).

Still another rhetorical device in the preacher's repertoire is his use of rhetorical questions. From what had been said and from the way in which the questions are asked, it is clear what answers the preacher expects. The first two questions (3:16 and 3:17) are answered by two more questions, while the final question (3:18) receives a response by means of a declarative sentence (3:19).

The first pair of questions (3:16) establish that those who had rebelled were those Israelites who came out of Egypt with Moses. Their disobedience is the main topic in Psalm 95:7b-11. The second pair of questions (3:17) indicate that God was angry with those people because they sinned in putting God to the test and in rebelling against God. The punishment for that generation's rebelliousness was death in the wilderness before any could enter "rest" in the land of Canaan (see Num 14:29-30).

The third question (3:18) affirms that God swore an oath against the disobedient Israelites, so that they could not enter his rest. And the concluding comment (3:19) attributes their failure to "lack of faith." The

if not to those who were disobedient? [19]And we see that they could not enter for lack of faith.

4 **The Sabbath Rest.** [1]Therefore, let us be on our guard while the promise of entering into his rest remains, that none of you seem to have failed. [2]For in fact we have received the good news just as they did. But the word that they heard did not profit them, for they were not united in faith with those who listened. [3]For we who believed enter into [that] rest, just as he has said:

"As I swore in my wrath,
'They shall not enter into my rest,' "
and yet his works were accomplished at the foundation of the world. [4]For he has spoken somewhere about the seventh day in this manner, "And God rested on the seventh day from all his works"; [5]and again, in the previously mentioned place, "They shall not enter into my rest." [6]Therefore, since it remains that some will enter into it, and those who formerly received the good news did not enter because of disobedience, [7]he

author has made two important rhetorical moves here. He has linked disobedience to lack of faith as effect and cause (see Num 14:22-23). And he has repeated the word "rest" several times, thus preparing the listener to ask whether it may refer to something beyond life in the land of Canaan.

4:1-13 The abiding promise of sabbath rest

Having explained Psalm 95:7b-11 in terms of the disobedience and lack of faith shown by the Exodus generation, the preacher in 4:1-2 moves to the congregation that he addresses ("Therefore, let us . . .") and tells them that God's promise of entering "rest" remains a possibility in the present. He warns them to be on guard lest they fail to have that promise brought to fulfillment. Like the Exodus generation, they have received the "good news" (the same word as "gospel"). Like the Exodus generation, they run the risk of failure if they do not respond in faith. What they should learn from the negative example of the Exodus generation is the pivotal importance of faith issuing in obedience. Only then can they hope to enjoy the "rest" that God has promised.

What is this "rest"? It is not simply life in the land of Canaan after the Exodus from Egypt. Indeed, it remains a present possibility for the early Christians as God's people ("we who believed"). To clarify the meaning of "rest," the author in 4:3-5 uses the Jewish interpretive technique of explaining one verse in Scripture by another linked to the first by a common word. Part of the author's main text has been Psalm 95:11: "As I swore in my wrath, / 'They shall not enter into my rest.'" Genesis 2:2 is another text that mentions "rest": "And God rested on the seventh day from all his works." The second text, of course, is from the biblical account of creation and expresses God's plan for creation. The combination of the two texts

once more set a day, "today," when long afterwards he spoke through David, as already quoted:

> "Oh, that today you would hear his voice:
> 'Harden not your hearts.' "

[8]Now if Joshua had given them rest, he would not have spoken afterwards of another day. [9]Therefore, a sabbath rest still remains for the people of God. [10]And whoever enters into God's rest, rests from his own works as God did from his. [11]Therefore, let us strive to enter into that rest, so that no one may fall after the same example of disobedience.

[12]Indeed, the word of God is living and effective, sharper than any two-edged sword, penetrating even between soul and spirit, joints and marrow, and able to discern reflections and thoughts of the heart. [13]No creature ▶

---

suggests that "rest" really refers to eternal life with God. The "rest" denied the Exodus generation was but a shadow of the rest that God has enjoyed since the beginning of creation and that God makes available to all who believe.

In 4:6-8 the author makes clear that God's promise of rest remains valid, despite the failure of the Exodus generation to attain to it because of their disobedience. The key word in this section is "today," which suggests that God's promise of rest remains a possibility even after the Exodus generation. Here the author works with the traditional ascription of the psalms to David (see 4:7). Now David lived long after Joshua, the one who finally did lead God's people into the promised land of Canaan. If Joshua had given genuine rest to God's people, David would not have been able to speak about "today" as the time to hear God's voice and so enjoy rest with God. In Greek the names Joshua and Jesus are the same. But the rest that God's people enjoyed under Joshua's leadership was but a shadow or type of the genuine rest that is now available to God's people through Jesus' leadership.

Finally, in 4:9-10 the author brings together what he has been saying about rest: "a sabbath rest still remains for the people of God" (4:9). This sabbath rest is God's own sabbath rest on the seventh day of creation (see Gen 2:2); it is not simply life in the land of Canaan or even observance of the sabbath day. Rather, it is sharing in God's sabbath rest, which began on the seventh day of creation and lasts forever. It is fullness of life with God.

And yet, as 4:11 makes clear, the enjoyment of God's own rest demands a deliberate choice ("let us strive to enter into that rest") to avoid the kind of disobedience displayed by the Exodus generation ("so that no one may fall").

is concealed from him, but everything is naked and exposed to the eyes of him to whom we must render an account.

Jesus, Compassionate High Priest. ◄ ¹⁴Therefore, since we have a great high priest who has passed through the heavens, Jesus, the Son of God, let us ◄ hold fast to our confession. ¹⁵For we do not have a high priest who is unable to sympathize with our weaknesses, but one who has similarly been tested in ◄ every way, yet without sin. ¹⁶So let us confidently approach the throne of grace to receive mercy and to find grace for timely help.

5 ¹Every high priest is taken from ► among men and made their representative before God, to offer gifts and sacrifices for sins. ²He is able to deal patiently with the ignorant and erring, for he himself is beset by weakness ³and ► so, for this reason, must make sin offerings for himself as well as for the people. ⁴No one takes this honor upon ► himself but only when called by God, just as Aaron was. ⁵In the same way, it

The preacher ends the first main part of his sermon in 4:12-13 with reflections on the word of God and the omniscience of God. The word of God (4:12) is more than the book we call the Bible. Because it comes from the living God, the word of God is living and active. Throughout his sermon thus far, the preacher has been concerned to show that the Scriptures can speak effectively to people in his own time. They are not simply witnesses to the past but rather have significance for "today." So effective are the Scriptures in addressing the concerns of people today that they can be compared to a sharp ("two-edged") sword that can penetrate into a person's inmost self ("between soul and spirit, joints and marrow") and can distinguish among thoughts and intentions.

In 4:13 the subject changes from the word of God to God ("him"), or more precisely, to the omniscience of God. Nothing can remain hidden from God. And to God everyone must be ready to render an accounting as to a judge. Thus the author seeks to motivate his congregation to strive ever more vigorously for eternal life with God ("rest") by reminding them of the possible consequences of not doing so.

THE PRIESTHOOD AND SACRIFICE OF CHRIST

Heb 4:14–10:18

4:14–5:10 Jesus as the compassionate high priest

The author began his sermon by establishing Jesus' identity as the Son of God. In the central section of his sermon, he will show how the Son of God is also the great high priest. The material in 4:14-16 serves as the link between the first two main sections, and enables the preacher to advance

was not Christ who glorified himself in becoming high priest, but rather the one who said to him:

"You are my son;
this day I have begotten you";

6just as he says in another place:

"You are a priest forever
according to the order of
Melchizedek."

7In the days when he was in the flesh, he offered prayers and supplications with loud cries and tears to the one who was able to save him from death, and he was heard because of his reverence. 8Son though he was, he learned obedience from what he suffered; 9and when he was made perfect, he became the source of eternal salvation for all who

---

his argument about the saving significance of Jesus' death and resurrection. The reuse of many of the same words and ideas in 10:19-23 will in turn enable him to round off (by the device of "inclusion") the second part and move to the third and final part.

True to his craft as a preacher, the author in 4:14-16 alternates between theological statements about Jesus' high priesthood (4:14a, 15) and exhortations ("let us . . . ," 4:14b, 16). The first theological statement (4:14a) must be understood against the background of the Jewish Day of Atonement ritual described in Leviticus 16. There the Jewish high priest is instructed to pass through the curtain in front of the Holy of Holies and to offer sacrifice on behalf of the sins of the people. But Jesus the Son of God "has passed through the heavens" in his resurrection and exaltation. Whereas the Jewish high priest entered only the earthly symbol of God's presence, Jesus has entered the real abode of God (heaven). More than anyone else, therefore, Jesus deserves the title of "great high priest." The first exhortation (4:14b) concerns perseverance in the confession of faith in the saving significance of Jesus' death "for us" and "for our sins."

The second theological statement (4:15) again takes as its premise an idea in Leviticus 16—that the high priest is a sinner and makes atonement for his own sins. Though Jesus was "without sin," he nonetheless experienced the moral and physical testing (see Mark 1:12-13; Matt 4:1-11; Luke 4:1-13) that is part of the human condition. As fully human, the Son of God can "sympathize with our weaknesses." The second exhortation (4:16) moves beyond "holding on" and urges the readers to approach God's throne with boldness. This confidence is based on the new relationship made possible through Jesus' activity as "our great high priest" in his sacrificial death and in his exaltation. While the motif of God's throne might imply judgment and condemnation, now through Christ it has become a "throne of grace" (a place of divine favor) from which one can expect mercy and grace from God. It is Christ who makes possible this

25

A panorama of the upper Galilee Valley

obey him, [10]declared by God high priest according to the order of Melchizedek.

IV. Jesus' Eternal Priesthood and Eternal Sacrifice

Exhortation to Spiritual Renewal. [11]About this we have much to say, and

it is difficult to explain, for you have become sluggish in hearing. [12]Although you should be teachers by this time, you need to have someone teach you again the basic elements of the utterances of God. You need milk, [and] not solid food. [13]Everyone who lives on

access to God's throne and this confident attitude among those who approach God.

But how can Jesus of Nazareth be called a high priest at all? In ancient Israel only men from the tribe of Levi who could trace their heritage back to Aaron were qualified to serve as high priests. As the author freely admits in 7:14, Jesus was descended from Judah and so had no earthly claim to the Jewish priesthood. The answer to the question resides in the different qualifications for priesthood developed in 5:1-10 and in the different priesthood explained in 7:1-28. (Note the reuse of terms from 5:1-3 in 7:27-28.) The intervening exhortation in 5:11–6:20 spells out the consequences of Jesus' different high priesthood for Christian life.

The high priest is first of all (5:1) a mediator between God and humans. As a human himself, he represents other humans before God, especially in his task of offering sacrifices for sins. Secondly (5:2-3), the high priest stands in solidarity with other humans because he shares their weakness. Thus he can show compassion to "the ignorant and erring." And as he offers the atoning sacrifices, he does so both for his own sins and for the sins of others. Thirdly (5:4), the high priest is called by God as Aaron was (see Exod 28:1) and does not take up the office on his own. More important than Aaronic/levitical descent for establishing Jesus' right to priesthood are the criteria of mediatorship, solidarity with others, and divine appointment. According to these criteria, it is possible to call Jesus "our great high priest."

The author applies these criteria in reverse (or chiastic) order. The divine appointment of Christ as high priest is established in 5:5-6 by means of quotations from the author's favorite biblical passages—Psalms 2 and 110. The author assumes that the speaker is God and the one addressed is Christ. Both psalms were used in coronation rituals for kings in ancient Israel, and so can be called "messianic." Since for the author and other early Christians the key to the Scriptures is Christ, these two oracles are understood to concern Christ. The first oracle (Ps 2:7 = Heb 5:5) establishes that Christ is God's Son (see Heb 1:5), and the second oracle (Ps 110:4 = Heb

milk lacks experience of the word of righteousness, for he is a child. [14]But solid food is for the mature, for those whose faculties are trained by practice to discern good and evil.

6 [1]Therefore, let us leave behind the basic teaching about Christ and advance to maturity, without laying the foundation all over again: repentance from dead works and faith in God, [2]instruction about baptisms and laying on of hands, resurrection of the dead and eternal judgment. [3]And we shall do this, if only God permits. [4]For it is impossible in the case of those who have once been enlightened and tasted the

---

5:6) introduces the idea (to be developed at great length in Hebrews 7) of the eternal priesthood of Christ "according to the order of Melchizedek." The two quotations interpreted from a christological perspective are put forward as proof that God has called and appointed Christ to be the great high priest.

Christ's solidarity with other humans is established in 5:7-8 by reference to his suffering—a universal human experience: "he learned obedience from what he suffered." The description of Christ's suffering most vividly evokes the episode in Gethsemane (see Mark 14:32-42; Matt 26:36-46; Luke 22:39-46) but probably also takes in all of his passion and death and indeed his entire life "in the flesh." The reference to his "prayers and supplications with loud cries and tears" places Jesus in the context of the many Old Testament lament psalms (see Psalms 3, 5, etc., and especially Psalm 22). From the author's christological perspective on biblical interpretation, Christ has become the speaker par excellence of the lament psalms. And in his case "because of his reverence" his prayers were heard, and he was vindicated through his resurrection and exaltation.

Christ's mediatorship, according to 5:9-10, surpasses that of any other priest: "when he was made perfect, he became the source of eternal salvation for all who obey him." The reference to Christ's being made perfect alludes to his having reached his "goal" through his death and resurrection, which in turn has made possible "eternal salvation for all who obey him." No other priest could bring about eternal salvation. The best that the Old Testament priests could do was the annual Day of Atonement ritual with its hope that the people's sins of the past year would be wiped away. The final verse (5:10) anticipates the full treatment of the different priesthood of Christ "according to the order of Melchizedek" in chapter 7.

5:11–6:12 A call to Christian maturity

Hebrews is not simply a theological treatise. It is a sermon that interweaves biblical exposition and theology with reflections on the spiritual

heavenly gift and shared in the holy Spirit ⁵and tasted the good word of God and the powers of the age to come, ⁶and then have fallen away, to bring them to repentance again, since they are recrucifying the Son of God for themselves and holding him up to contempt. ⁷Ground that has absorbed the rain falling upon it repeatedly and brings forth crops useful to those for whom it is cultivated receives a blessing from God. ⁸But if it produces thorns and thistles, it is rejected; it will soon be cursed and finally burned.

⁹But we are sure in your regard, beloved, of better things related to salvation, even though we speak in this way. ¹⁰For God is not unjust so as to overlook your work and the love you have demonstrated for his name by having served and continuing to serve the holy ones. ¹¹We earnestly desire each of you to demonstrate the same eagerness for the fulfillment of hope until the end, ¹²so that you may not become sluggish, but imitators of those who, through faith and patience, are inheriting the promises.

---

condition of the audience. Between his discussions of Christ's high priesthood in 4:14–5:10 and 7:1-28, the author issues a call to spiritual maturity (5:11–6:12) and offers an assurance about God's promises (6:13-20).

The call to Christian maturity in 5:11–6:12 consists of a reprimand (5:11–6:3), a stern warning (6:4-8), and a word of hope and encouragement (6:9-12). In the first part of the reprimand (5:11-14) the author admits that his topic of Christ's priesthood is "difficult to explain." But he locates the difficulty not so much in the material but rather in the audience ("you have become sluggish in hearing"). He goes on in 5:12 to scold them for failing to advance in Christian life. By this time they should have become teachers but in fact they stand in need of learning again the basic elements (the ABCs) of Christian faith. They remain in Christian infancy: "You need milk, [and] not solid food." In 5:13-14 he develops the contrast between the spiritually immature as lacking "experience of the word of righteousness" and the spiritually mature who can "discern good and evil." The Christian ideal is the integration of doctrine and practice.

The second part of the reprimand (6:1-3) challenges the congregation to move forward in their theological education and practice. The author urges them not to remain at the basic level, without of course neglecting the basics entirely—no more than one can neglect one's ABCs in writing or reading. The list of basics in 6:1b-2 is founded on "repentance from dead works and faith in God." Initiation into Christian life is covered by "baptisms and laying on of hands," while life-after-death is treated in "resurrection of the dead and eternal judgment." As they became Christians, the members of the congregation learned the distinctively Christian

◄ **God's Promise Immutable.** [13]When God made the promise to Abraham, since he had no one greater by whom to swear, "he swore by himself," [14] and said, "I will indeed bless you and multiply" you. [15]And so, after patient waiting, he obtained the promise. [16]Human beings swear by someone greater than themselves; for them an oath serves as a guarantee and puts an end to all argument. [17]So when God wanted to give the heirs of his promise an even clearer demonstration of the immutability of his purpose, he intervened with an oath, [18]so that by two immutable things, in which it was im-

---

interpretations of Jewish beliefs and practices. Even though they seemed to be wavering about these matters, the author hopes that by moving them forward to "advanced" teaching about Christ's priesthood and sacrifice all these issues will fall into place again for them. As a good preacher, however, he acknowledges in 6:3 that their progress depends ultimately on God ("if only God permits").

The stern warning in 6:4-8 (see 10:26-31) is intended to shock the community into recognizing the seriousness of turning aside from Christian faith. The author declares that repentance after apostasy is impossible for those who have been "enlightened and tasted the heavenly gift and shared in the holy Spirit"—a general description of Christian initiation (which need not be broken down into the separate sacraments of baptism, Eucharist, and confirmation)—and "tasted the good word of God and the powers of the age to come"—a reference to God's word encountered in the Old Testament and in the preached gospel and to the signs and wonders that were part of early Christian experience. Those who fall away from Christian faith are said to be recrucifying the Son of God and holding him up to contempt. The theology of this stern warning seems to be that since Christ's death has made possible the forgiveness of sins, those who reject its saving significance have nowhere else to go for repentance and forgiveness. The rhetorical force of the warning seeks to awaken the community to recognize the seriousness of their situation.

The stark choice that is before the community is illustrated in 6:7-8 by the contrast between the good soil and the bad soil (see Mark 4:3-9; Matt 13:3-9; Luke 8:4-8). Whereas the good soil that produces useful crops receives a blessing from God (see Gen 1:11-12), the bad soil that produces only thorns and thistles is cursed (see Gen 3:17-18) and burned off. This dramatic contrast underscores how serious a decision lay before the wavering Christians. Will they produce good fruits and be blessed by God in Christ? Or will they produce thorns and thistles, and so share in the curse imposed upon Adam?

possible for God to lie, we who have taken refuge might be strongly encouraged to hold fast to the hope that lies before us. [19]This we have as an anchor of the soul, sure and firm, which reaches into the interior behind the veil, [20]where Jesus has entered on our behalf as forerunner, becoming high priest forever according to the order of Melchizedek.

Having gotten the congregation's attention by his stern warning, the preacher in 6:9-12 offers some mitigating words of hope and encouragement. He first expresses in 6:9-10 confidence that his dear friends will enjoy the "better things related to salvation" because God will surely recognize their good works and the love that they have shown in serving their fellow Christians ("the holy ones"). Then in 6:11-12 he expresses his personal solicitude ("we earnestly desire") that they will persevere and so come to the fullness of what they can hope for in Christ. The stern warning of 6:4-8 has been replaced by the soothing talk of 6:9-12. But as the final comments in 6:12 indicate, the problem of spiritual sluggishness remains. If they are to enjoy what God has promised, they need to imitate the faith and patience shown by their spiritual forebears—a theme developed at length in Hebrews 11.

6:13-20 An assurance about God's promises

The reference to "inheriting the promises" in 6:12 provides the occasion for an assurance about God's promises in 6:13-20, which in turn prepares for the reflection in 7:1-28 about God's promise of a priest "according to the order of Melchizedek" in Psalm 110:4.

The key biblical text in the assurance is Genesis 22:16-17 in which God, impressed by Abraham's willingness to sacrifice his son Isaac, promises to Abraham many descendants. The two key points in the text for the author of Hebrews according to 6:13-15 are the content of the promise and the oath formula by which it is introduced ("he swore by himself"). The content of the promise is " 'I will indeed bless you and multiply' you." The oath formula is distinctive precisely because God "swore by himself." And the result is that Abraham obtained the promise "after patient waiting"— mostly likely not through Isaac alone but superabundantly through Christ.

In 6:16-18 the preacher continues his reflection on the oath and the promise of Genesis 22:16-17. In 6:16 he sets forth two basic principles of law: We humans customarily swear an oath by someone greater ("so help me God"), and we use an oath to end an argument ("I swear to God"). Then in 6:17-18 he refers back to Genesis 22:16-17 to make the case that God's promise is based not only on the content of the promise itself but

7 **Melchizedek, a Type of Christ.** ¹This "Melchizedek, king of Salem and priest of God Most High," "met Abraham as he returned from his defeat of the kings" and "blessed him." ²And Abraham apportioned to him "a tenth of everything." His name first means righteous king, and he was also "king of Salem," that is, king of peace. ³Without father, mother, or ancestry, without beginning of days or end of life, thus made to resemble the Son of God, he remains a priest forever.

⁴See how great he is to whom the patriarch "Abraham [indeed] gave a tenth" of his spoils. ⁵The descendants of Levi who receive the office of priesthood have a commandment according to the law to exact tithes from the people, that is, from their brothers, although they also have come from the loins of Abraham. ⁶But he who was not of their ancestry received tithes from Abraham and blessed him who had received the promises. ⁷Unquestionably, a lesser person is blessed by a greater. ⁸In the one case, mortal men receive tithes; in the other, a man of whom it is testified that he lives on. ⁹One might even say that Levi himself, who receives

also on the oath that precedes it. We can trust God's promise to Abraham and his descendants (in Christ) because it is based on "two immutable things"—God's word and God's oath. The significance of these reflections will become clearer in the meditation on Psalm 110:4 in chapter 7.

The final two verses (6:19-20) bring the listeners back to the topic of the high priesthood of Christ, which will be treated at length in chapter 7. They also introduce two striking images. God's promise fulfilled in Christ is "an anchor of the soul" (6:19), and Jesus is the "forerunner"—the leader who has gone before us to eternal life with God (6:20). As the high priest of Leviticus 16 entered the Holy of Holies on the Day of Atonement, so Christ has gone before us to enter God's heavenly court.

7:1-28 Jesus as a priest according to the order of Melchizedek

After moving from the first reflection on Christ's priesthood in 4:14–5:10 to exhortation in 5:11–6:20, the author returns to his main theological topic: Jesus' priesthood according to the order of Melchizedek.

In the Old Testament Melchizedek appears only in Genesis 14:17-20 and Psalm 110:4. These two passages will serve as the biblical basis for the author's argument about the superiority and eternal character of the priesthood of Christ. Although there were some speculations about Melchizedek in early Jewish and Christian writings, here the author is concerned only with establishing his points on the basis of these two biblical texts. How he handles them reveals much about Jewish biblical interpretation in the first century A.D. and about the Christian conviction that Christ is the key to the Scriptures.

tithes, was tithed through Abraham, [10]for he was still in his father's loins when Melchizedek met him.

[11]If, then, perfection came through the levitical priesthood, on the basis of which the people received the law, what need would there still have been for another priest to arise according to the order of Melchizedek, and not reckoned according to the order of Aaron? [12]When there is a change of priesthood, there is necessarily a change of law as well. [13]Now he of whom these things are said belonged to a different tribe, of which no member ever officiated at the altar. [14]It is clear that our Lord arose from Judah, and in regard to that tribe Moses said nothing about priests. [15]It is even more obvious if another priest is raised up after the likeness of Melchizedek, [16]who has become so, not by a law expressed in a commandment concerning physical descent but by the power of a life that cannot be destroyed. [17]For it is testified:

"You are a priest forever
according to the order of
Melchizedek."

[18]On the one hand, a former commandment is annulled because of its weakness

---

The reflection on Genesis 14:17-20 in Hebrews 7:1-10 seeks to show the superiority of Christ's priesthood to the Jewish levitical priesthood. In 7:1-2a the author introduces Melchizedek as "king of Salem and priest of God Most High" and focuses on the two matters of greatest importance to his argument: Melchizedek blessed Abraham as he returned from battle, and Abraham gave to Melchizedek a tithe or "tenth of everything."

In 7:2b-3 the author considers the person of Melchizedek. His name can be interpreted in Hebrew to mean "king of righteousness" or "righteous king." Likewise, the name of his city "Salem" (which was most likely Jerusalem) can be associated with the Hebrew word for "peace." As righteous king and king of peace, Melchizedek was a type of Christ. Moreover, in Genesis 14:17-20 Melchizedek comes out of nowhere. He is given no genealogy ("without father, mother, or ancestry"), and nothing is said about his birth or death ("without beginning of days or end of life"). This argument from silence contributes to the author's case that Melchizedek prefigures Jesus the Son of God. But the real focus of attention is the superior priesthood of Melchizedek and Christ.

The rest of the argument on the basis of Genesis 14:17-20 in 7:4-10 focuses on the acts of blessing and tithing. By Jewish custom the superior figure blesses the inferior figure. By Jewish custom all the other tribes pay a tithe or tax to support the priestly tribe of Levi (see Num 18:21-24). But according to Genesis 14:17-20 Abraham gave a tenth of all his spoils (a tithe) to Melchizedek, who had blessed Abraham. Both actions show the superiority of Melchizedek to Abraham. Since the patriarch Levi—from

and uselessness, [19]for the law brought nothing to perfection; on the other hand, a better hope is introduced, through which we draw near to God. [20]And to the degree that this happened not without the taking of an oath—for others became priests without an oath, [21]but he with an oath, through the one who said to him:

"The Lord has sworn, and he will not repent:
'You are a priest forever' "— [22]to that same degree has Jesus [also] become the guarantee of an [even] better covenant. [23]Those priests were many because they were prevented by death from remaining in office, [24]but ▶ he, because he remains forever, has a

---

whom the Jewish levitical priests traced their lineage—was a descendant of Abraham, these two actions, according to the reasoning of the author of Hebrews, suggest the anteriority and superiority of Melchizedek's priesthood to that of Levi. It is as if Levi, before he was born, had already acknowledged the superiority of Melchizedek and so of Christ. The next step in the argument is to prove that Christ's priesthood is the priesthood of Melchizedek.

The reflection on Psalm 110:4 in Hebrews 7:11-28 seeks to establish the eternal character of Christ's priesthood. The text is quoted in 7:17: "You are a priest forever / according to the order of Melchizedek." The oracle is introduced by an oath formula, which is quoted in 7:21: "The Lord has sworn, and he will not repent: / 'You are a priest . . .'" The author contends that the promise (ratified by an oath) of an eternal priesthood in Psalm 110:4 has been fulfilled in Christ.

Having established the anteriority and superiority of Melchizedek's priesthood in 7:1-10, the author now argues that the priesthood of Melchizedek has found its fulfillment in Christ, and that Christ's priesthood has superseded that of Levi. Whereas the events described in Gen 14:17-20 preceded chronologically the law of Moses and the levitical priesthood, the oracle in Psalm 110:4 (whose origin in David's time is assumed) came later than the law of Moses and the levitical priesthood.

In 7:11 the author reasons that if the levitical priesthood brought "perfection" (see 7:28), there would have been no need for God to promise another priesthood in Psalm 110:4. He observes in 7:12 that a change of priesthood implies a change of law. This is part of his argument that Christ represents better promises and a better covenant.

There was, however, an obvious obstacle to calling Jesus a priest in a Jewish context. Jesus did not belong to the priestly tribe of Levi. Rather, he belonged to the royal tribe of Judah through King David. The author freely admits this fact in 7:13-14. How then could Jesus be called a priest?

33

priesthood that does not pass away. ²⁵Therefore, he is always able to save those who approach God through him, since he lives forever to make intercession for them.

²⁶It was fitting that we should have such a high priest: holy, innocent, undefiled, separated from sinners, higher than the heavens. ²⁷He has no need, as did the high priests, to offer sacrifice day after day, first for his own sins and then for those of the people; he did that once for all when he offered himself. ²⁸For the law appoints men subject to weakness to be high priests, but the word of the oath, which was taken after the law, appoints a son, who has been made perfect forever.

This was made possible through Jesus' resurrection from the dead. Jesus became a priest "by the power of a life that cannot be destroyed" (7:16), thus fulfilling the promise of an eternal priesthood ("forever") in Psalm 110:4. His priesthood replaced the weak and imperfect priesthood of Levi. Because Christ's priesthood has provided an access to God that was impossible under the old priesthood, it has introduced "a better hope" (7:18-19), which is eternal life with God.

The eternal priesthood of Christ is based according to 7:20-22 not only on the promise of God ("You are a priest forever") but also on the oath of God ("The Lord has sworn, and he will not repent"). At this point the author builds on his reflections about two immutable things—God's promise and God's oath—in 6:13-20. Just as Christ's priesthood means "a change of law" (7:12) and "a better hope" (7:19), so it is also "the guarantee of an [even] better covenant" (7:22). The levitical priesthood was not eternal, since the levitical priests died (7:23). But since the risen Christ lives forever, his priesthood is eternal (7:24) and so is "always" able to make intercession with God (which is what priests do) for "those who approach God through him" (7:25).

The concluding reflection in 7:26-28 highlights the heavenly character of Christ's priesthood. He is "holy, innocent, undefiled, separated from sinners, higher than the heavens" (7:26). His death on the cross represents the one, perfect sacrifice. And so he has no need to offer sacrifices every day for his own sins and the sins of others. In describing the perfect sacrifice of Christ in 7:27 the author summarizes the theology of his entire work: "he did that once for all when he offered himself." Christ is both the priest (the one who offers sacrifice) and the victim (what is offered), and his sacrifice has value "once for all." There is no need for other sacrifices or other priests in the light of Jesus' one, perfect sacrifice.

The final verse (7:28) argues for the superiority and eternal character of Christ's priesthood on three counts. Whereas the law merely "appoints"

The ruins of a synagogue in Israel

8 **Heavenly Priesthood of Jesus.** ¹The main point of what has been said is this: we have such a high priest, who has taken his seat at the right hand of the throne of the Majesty in heaven, ²a minister of the sanctuary and of the true tabernacle that the Lord, not man, set up. ³Now every high priest is appointed to offer gifts and sacrifices; thus the necessity for this one also to have something to offer. ⁴If then he were on earth, he would not be a priest, since there are those who offer gifts according to the law. ⁵They worship in a copy and shadow of the heavenly sanctuary, as Moses was warned when he was about to erect the tabernacle. For he says, "See that you make everything according to the pattern shown you on the mountain." ⁶Now he has obtained

---

high priests, the oracle about Christ's priesthood in Psalm 110:4 is accompanied by a divine oath. Whereas the levitical high priests were subject to "weakness," the risen Christ is the Son of God "made perfect forever." Whereas the levitical priesthood was part of the law of Moses, Christ's priesthood which came later than the law not only with regard to Christ but also to Psalm 110:4 is the key to the better covenant—the primary topic of chapter 8.

8:1-6 Jesus' heavenly priesthood

Having established the eternal character of Christ's priesthood on the basis of Psalm 110:4, the author argues that the place of Christ's priesthood and sacrifice is heaven. As a good preacher, he offers in 8:1 both a recapitulation ("we have such a [great] high priest") and a transition to the next topic (heaven as the locus of Christ's priestly ministry). Here Psalm 110:1 ("The LORD said to my Lord: `Sit at my right hand . . .'"), which was already cited in 1:13 (see also 1:3), serves as one starting point. The other starting point is the early Christian belief that Jesus, having really died, was raised from the dead and now lives with God in glory ("at the right hand of the throne of the Majesty in heaven").

The two main topics of 8:2-5 are the sanctuary and the sacrifices associated with Christ's priesthood. The sanctuary where Christ ministers has been established by God, not by human beings. It is therefore the "true tabernacle" in the sense that every earthly sanctuary is a copy and shadow of the heavenly sanctuary. This theme is developed in 8:5.

Before that, however, the author must treat in 8:3-4 the heavenly nature of Christ's sacrifices. If Christ were on earth, he would not be offering sacrifices since by the definition of the law of Moses he would not be a priest (because he was from the tribe of Judah, not of Levi). But of course, the sacrifice of Christ was his own self in his death on the cross. Those

31:32 *(handwritten)*

so much more excellent a ministry as he is mediator of a better covenant, enacted on better promises.

Old and New Covenants. ⁷For if that first covenant had been faultless, no place would have been sought for a second one. ⁸But he finds fault with them and says:

"Behold, the days are coming, says the Lord,

31:31 *(handwritten)*

    when I will conclude a new covenant with the house of Israel and the house of Judah.

⁹It will not be like the covenant I
    made with their fathers
    the day I took them by the hand
      to lead them forth from
      the land of Egypt;
for they did not stand by my
    covenant
    and I ignored them, says the
      Lord.

31:33 *(handwritten)*

¹⁰But this is the covenant I will establish with the house of Israel after those days, says the Lord:
I will put my laws in their minds
    and I will write them upon their
      hearts.

QUOTE FROM JEREMIAH 31:31 *(handwritten)*

priests who function on earth do so at an earthly sanctuary and offer earthly gifts and sacrifices to God. Their sanctuary is only "a copy and shadow of the heavenly sanctuary" (8:5).

Such language is reminiscent of Plato's teaching that the visible world is but a copy and shadow of the ideal world. A more likely source, however, is God's instruction to Moses in Exodus 25:40 when Moses began to construct the tabernacle: "See that you make everything according to the pattern shown you on the mountain." The idea is that God gave Moses a "blueprint" or prototype of the tabernacle on Mount Sinai. The heavenly sanctuary of Christ's priesthood is "the real thing," and other sanctuaries are at best poor imitations. Since the author had already established the "better promises" and the "more excellent" character of Christ's ministry, 8:6 functions as another summary. It also serves as a transition, since it introduces the theme of a "better covenant."

8:7-13 The old and new covenants

This section contains the longest continuous Old Testament quotation in the New Testament. The text is the prophecy of God's new covenant with his people that appears in Jeremiah 31:31-34. The historical background is the prophet's recognition that soon Jerusalem and its temple would be captured and destroyed by the Babylonians in the early sixth century B.C. While often described as a prophet of doom, Jeremiah was also a prophet of hope. His hope was based on God's fidelity to his people and to his promises, not on the strength of Judah's armies and kings. His prophecy of a new covenant looks forward to a restored and superior

I will be their God,
and they shall be my people.
[11]And they shall not teach, each one his fellow citizen
and kinsman, saying, 'Know the Lord,'
for all shall know me,
from least to greatest.
[12]For I will forgive their evildoing
and remember their sins no
more."

31:34

END QUOTE

[13]When he speaks of a "new" covenant, he declares the first one obsolete. And what has become obsolete and has grown old is close to disappearing.

9 The Worship of the First Covenant. [1]Now [even] the first covenant had regulations for worship and an earthly sanctuary. [2]For a tabernacle was constructed, the outer one, in which were the lampstand, the table,

relationship between God and Israel, one more perfect than anything that Israel had yet experienced.

The author in 8:7 introduces the quotation by observing that if the first covenant had been perfect and without blemish, there would have been no need for a second or new covenant. At this point and 8:13, his only explicit interest is with the word "new" in the promise of a new covenant. Nevertheless, there are other themes in Jeremiah 31:31-34 that are also important, especially the ideas of God's renewed relationship with Israel, the internal appropriation of the new covenant ("in their minds . . . upon their hearts"), and the forgiveness of sins.

The concluding comment in 8:13 explores the implications of the "new" covenant. Such language, according to the author, makes the first covenant "obsolete." He goes on to qualify that strong term by explaining that "what has become obsolete and has grown old is close to disappearing." That was the perspective of the prophet Jeremiah, for he recognized the catastrophe that would soon fall upon Judah in the early sixth century B.C. Is it also the perspective of the author of Hebrews? If so, to what does he refer? Could it be the Jerusalem temple (which was destroyed in A.D. 70), the institutions of the Old Testament (priesthood, sanctuary, sacrifices, etc.), or Judaism in general? Why are they said to be "close to disappearing," instead of already "disappeared"?

9:1-10 The earthly sanctuary

Having argued that the sanctuary of Christ's priesthood is in heaven, the author explains that the earthly sanctuary described in Exodus 25–26 was a shadow or "parable" of the real thing. He also prepares for the characterization of Christ's perfect sacrifice in 9:11–10:18 in terms of the rituals of the Day of Atonement (Leviticus 16).

and the bread of offering; this is called the Holy Place. ³Behind the second veil was the tabernacle called the Holy of Holies, ⁴in which were the gold altar of incense and the ark of the covenant entirely covered with gold. In it were the gold jar containing the manna, the staff of Aaron that had sprouted, and the tablets of the covenant. ⁵Above it were the cherubim of glory overshadowing the place of expiation. Now is not the time to speak of these in detail.

⁶With these arrangements for worship, the priests, in performing their service, go into the outer tabernacle repeatedly, ⁷but the high priest alone goes into the inner one once a year, not without blood that he offers for himself and for the sins of the people. ⁸In this way the holy Spirit shows that the way into the sanctuary had not yet been revealed while the outer tabernacle still had its place. ⁹This is a symbol of the present time, in which gifts and sacrifices are offered that cannot perfect the worshiper in conscience ¹⁰but only in matters of food and drink and various ritual washings: regulations concerning the flesh, imposed until the time of the new order.

The "earthly sanctuary" of the first covenant is described in 9:1-5 in terms of its "regulations" (which in 9:10 are called "regulations concerning the flesh"). Taking his information from Exodus 25–26, the author first in 9:2 mentions the outer tent or tabernacle, with its furnishings consisting of the lamp-stand, the table, and the bread of offering. The name of the outer tent is "the Holy Place." The inner tent is called "the Holy of Holies," the place where only the high priest could enter once a year on the Day of Atonement (9:3-5). Its furnishings—the gold altar of incense, the gilded ark of the covenant, a gold jar containing manna, Aaron's staff, and the tablets of God's covenant with Moses—are more exotic and elaborate than those of the Holy Place. The list is drawn from the book of Exodus and from popular traditions, not necessarily from the realities of the Second Temple. The most important feature of the inner tent, however, is "the place of expiation" (often translated as "the mercy seat"), the place in the Holy of Holies that was sprinkled with blood by the high priest on the Day of Atonement (see Lev 16:14-15; Rom 3:25). Recognizing that prolonging these descriptions might lead to distraction, the author in 9:5 abruptly breaks off his treatment ("now is not the time . . .").

To highlight further the importance of the rituals of the Day of Atonement, the preacher in 9:6-7 contrasts what happened in the outer tent and what happened in the inner tent. Whereas in the Holy Place many priests repeatedly performed their sacrifices for sins, only the high priest might enter the Holy of Holies once a year for the purpose of sprinkling blood there "for himself and for the sins of the people."

Sacrifice of Jesus. [11]But when Christ came as high priest of the good things that have come to be, passing through the greater and more perfect tabernacle not made by hands, that is, not belonging to this creation, [12]he entered once for all into the sanctuary, not with the blood of goats and calves but with his own blood, thus obtaining eternal redemption. [13]For if the blood of goats and bulls and the sprinkling of a heifer's ashes can sanctify those who are defiled so that their flesh is cleansed, [14]how much more will the blood of Christ, who through the eternal spirit offered himself unblemished to God, cleanse our consciences from dead works to worship the living God.

[15]For this reason he is mediator of a new covenant: since a death has taken place for deliverance from transgressions under the first covenant, those who are called may receive the promised eternal inheritance. [16]Now where there is a will, the death of the testator must be established. [17]For a will takes effect only

---

However important the rituals of the Day of Atonement might seem, they were inadequate when compared with the perfect sacrifice of Christ (9:8-10). These institutions of the old covenant were used by the holy Spirit to foreshadow the genuine "way into the sanctuary" that Christ the high priest would reveal (9:8). They belonged to "the present time" and could not perfect persons in the depth of their being ("in conscience"). They were "regulations concerning the flesh" that were in force "until the time of the new order" or "the age to come" that has been inaugurated by Christ's life, death, resurrection, and exaltation. They functioned as symbols or parables, dealt with earthly things (food, drink, ablutions, etc.), were open to only a select few (the priests), and were imperfect by nature. They pointed to the perfect sacrifice of Christ offered in his death on the cross for us and for our sins.

9:11-28 The efficacy of Christ's blood

The essence of the Day of Atonement ritual was the high priest's sprinkling of animal blood inside the Holy of Holies. Based on the idea of blood as a symbol of life and as an agent of purification, this action was believed to take away the past sins of the people (including those of the high priest himself) and to prepare them for renewed life before God in the new year. For the author of Hebrews, Christ is both the perfect high priest and the perfect sacrifice (in his death on the cross). His blood, shed only once, accomplished what the blood of animals shed annually could not achieve.

In 9:11-14 the author affirms that Christ the "high priest of the good things that have come to be" ("the age to come," which is already here) has entered the divinely constructed tent (heaven) with his own blood

at death; it has no force while the testator is alive. [18]Thus not even the first covenant was inaugurated without blood. [19]When every commandment had been proclaimed by Moses to all the people according to the law, he took the blood of calves [and goats], together with water and crimson wool and hyssop, and sprinkled both the book itself and all the people, [20]saying, "This is 'the blood of the covenant which God has enjoined upon you.'" [21]In the same way, he sprinkled also the tabernacle and all the vessels of worship with blood. [22]According to the law almost everything is purified by blood, and without the shedding of blood there is no forgiveness.

[23]Therefore, it was necessary for the copies of the heavenly things to be purified by these rites, but the heavenly things themselves by better sacrifices than these. [24]For Christ did not enter into a sanctuary made by hands, a copy of the true one, but heaven itself, that he might now appear before God on our behalf. [25]Not that he might offer himself repeatedly, as the high priest enters each year into the sanctuary with blood that is not his own; [26]if that were so, he would have had to suffer repeatedly from the foundation of the world. But now once for all he has appeared at the end of the ages to take away sin by his sacrifice. [27]Just as it is appointed that human beings die once, and after this the judgment, [28]so also Christ, offered once to take away the sins of many, will appear a second time, not to take away sin but to bring salvation to those who eagerly await him.

(not animal blood) as the perfect sacrifice offered once for all, with "eternal redemption" as its result. He celebrates the greater efficacy of Christ's sacrifice by arguing in 9:13-14 "from the lesser to the greater." If the animal blood used in earthly sacrifices had any efficacy with regard to the body, how much more has Christ's perfect sacrifice on the cross ("the blood of Christ") cleansed consciences from sins and made it possible to worship the living God. By entering the heavenly sanctuary with his blood, Christ provided an effective cleansing from sin and made possible right relationship with God (what Paul calls "justification").

In 9:15-22 the author contends that the blood of Christ has inaugurated the new covenant prophesied by Jeremiah. Christ is the mediator of that new covenant through his death on the cross (9:15). To explain this point in 9:16-17, he plays on the double meaning of "testament," which can refer to a "covenant" and to a "last will and testament." Just as a last will is activated only when the person dies, so the promise of the new covenant has been activated through the death of Christ. The result is redemption from sins under the old covenant and participation in the eternal inheritance. Just as the old covenant given to Moses on Sinai was ratified by the sprinkling of blood upon an altar (see Exod 24:3-8), so the new covenant has been ratified by the shedding of Christ's blood on the cross. In 9:22 the author describes

10 **One Sacrifice instead of Many.** [1]Since the law has only a shadow of the good things to come, and not the very image of them, it can never make perfect those who come to worship by the same sacrifices that they offer continually each year. [2]Otherwise, would not the sacrifices have ceased to be offered, since the worshipers, once cleansed, would no longer have had any consciousness of sins? [3]But in those sacrifices there is only a yearly remembrance of sins, [4]for it is impossible that the blood of bulls and goats take away sins. [5]For this reason, when he came into the world, he said:

> "Sacrifice and offering you did not
>   desire,
>   but a body you prepared for me;
> [6]holocausts and sin offerings you
>   took no delight in.
> [7]Then I said, 'As is written of me in
>   the scroll,
> Behold, I come to do your will, O
>   God.' "

[8]First he says, "Sacrifices and offerings, holocausts and sin offerings, you neither desired nor delighted in." These are offered according to the law. [9]Then he says, "Behold, I come to do your

blood as a means of purification and of forgiveness, and observes that "without the shedding of blood there is no forgiveness" (see Lev 17:11).

In 9:23-28 the author argues that by approaching God in the heavenly sanctuary with his own blood Christ brought about a complete purification of sins. But Christ's work is not simply a past event ("once for all," see 9:12). Rather, Christ the high priest continues to exercise a priestly ministry in heaven: "that he might now appear before God on our behalf" (9:24). Moreover, Christ the high priest will exercise a priestly ministry at the last judgment when he "will appear a second time" (9:28). Since he has already taken away sins by his death on the cross, then his task will be "to bring salvation to those who eagerly await him." Thus there are three phases in the priestly work of Christ: cleansing from sin (past), ongoing mediation on our behalf (present), and final deliverance (future).

10:1-18 Christ as the effective priest and sacrifice

As he reaches the close of his reflections on the priesthood and sacrifice of Christ, the author in 10:1-4 insists that the repeated sacrifices under the law of Moses were ineffective. At best they were "a shadow of the good things to come" as opposed to the true form or image, and so they were incapable of making perfect those who offered them at the Day of Atonement (10:1). The very fact that these sacrifices were repeated every year shows their inability to bring about real atonement for sins (10:2-3). Finally the author asserts in 10:4 that the blood of bulls and goats cannot take away sins.

will." He takes away the first to establish the second. ¹⁰By this "will," we have been consecrated through the offering of the body of Jesus Christ once for all.

¹¹Every priest stands daily at his ministry, offering frequently those same sacrifices that can never take away sins. ¹²But this one offered one sacrifice for sins, and took his seat forever at the right hand of God; ¹³now he waits until his enemies are made his footstool. ¹⁴For by one offering he has made perfect forever those who are being consecrated. ¹⁵The holy Spirit also testifies to us, for after saying:

> ¹⁶"This is the covenant I will establish with them after those days, says the Lord:
> 'I will put my laws in their hearts, and I will write them upon their minds,' "

¹⁷he also says:

> "Their sins and their evildoing I will remember no more."

¹⁸Where there is forgiveness of these, there is no longer offering for sin.

Next in 10:5-10 the author contends that the many sacrifices offered according to the law of Moses have been superseded by the one perfect sacrifice of Christ. To make this point he places the words of Psalm 40:5-7 in the mouth of Christ "when he came into the world" (the incarnation) as a statement of Christ's vocation and the superiority of his sacrifice. In 10:8 the author identifies the sacrifices of Psalm 40 with those offered according to the law of Moses. Then in 10:9-10 he goes on to contrast those sacrifices with the one perfect sacrifice of Christ's body offered on the cross. His sacrifice has superseded and even abolished the animal sacrifices. Only the one perfect sacrifice of Jesus Christ was able to make people holy ("consecrated"). That sacrifice was offered in a spirit of faithful obedience to God's will: "Behold I come to do your will."

Just as the many sacrifices under the law have been superseded by the one sacrifice of Christ, so according to 10:11-14 the many priests have been replaced by the one priest. Under the law of Moses there were many priests who offered the same sacrifices over and over without being able to take away sins (10:11). However, Christ the one great high priest "offered one sacrifice for sins" (in his death on the cross) and has been exalted to God's right hand (Jesus' resurrection and ascension, described in terms of Ps 110:1). The one perfect sacrifice of Christ is summarized as follows: "For by one offering he has made perfect forever those who are being consecrated."

Whereas the repeated sacrifices by the priests of the old covenant were ineffective, the one sacrifice of Christ the priest of the new covenant

Recalling the Past. [19]Therefore, brothers, since through the blood of Jesus we have confidence of entrance into the sanctuary [20]by the new and living way he opened for us through the veil, that is, his flesh, [21]and since we have "a great priest over the house of God," [22]let us approach with a sincere heart and in absolute trust, with our hearts sprinkled clean from an evil conscience and our bodies washed in pure water. [23]Let us hold unwaveringly to our confession that gives us hope, for he who made the promise is trustworthy. [24]We must consider how to rouse one another to love and good works. [25]We should not stay away from our assembly, as is the custom of some, but encourage one another, and this all the more as you see the day drawing near.

[26]If we sin deliberately after receiving knowledge of the truth, there no longer remains sacrifice for sins [27]but a fearful prospect of judgment and a flaming fire that is going to consume the adversaries. [28]Anyone who rejects

brings about the forgiveness of sins. The motif of the new covenant is introduced by quotations from Jeremiah 31:31-34 in 10:15-17. The new covenant that is inscribed on hearts and minds matches the total interior obedience of Christ ("I come to do your will"). The new covenant wipes away sins and allows God's people to make a new start. So effective is the one perfect sacrifice of Christ in forgiving sins that there is no need for any more sacrifices: "Where there is forgiveness of these, there is no longer offering for sin" (10:18). Thus the sacrificial system of the old covenant, which was at best a "shadow" of Christ's sacrifice, has been superseded. From now on the forgiveness of sins is necessarily linked to Jesus' sacrificial death for us and for our sins. Other sacrifices have been rendered unnecessary.

PERSEVERANCE IN CHRISTIAN LIFE

Heb 10:19–13:25

10:19-39 A call to persevere in faith

Following a pattern set in 5:11–6:12, this passage consists of an appeal (10:19-25), a stern warning (10:26-31), and a word of encouragement (10:32-39). It ends on a note of faith, which prepares for the catalogue of the heroes of faith in chapter 11.

Using language reminiscent of 4:14-16, the author in 10:19-21 provides a theological foundation for his appeal by affirmations about what has happened through Jesus' death, resurrection, and exaltation. Through the blood of Christ we have access to the heavenly sanctuary and have a great high priest who mediates with God on our behalf. The three appeals in

A Jew praying at the Western Wall in Jerusalem

the law of Moses is put to death without pity on the testimony of two or three witnesses. ²⁹Do you not think that a much worse punishment is due the one who has contempt for the Son of God, considers unclean the covenant-blood by which he was consecrated, and insults the spirit of grace? ³⁰We know the one who said:

"Vengeance is mine; I will repay,"

and again:

"The Lord will judge his people." (³¹It is a fearful thing to fall into the hands of the living God.)

³²Remember the days past when, after you had been enlightened, you endured a great contest of suffering. ³³At times you were publicly exposed to abuse and affliction; at other times you associated yourselves with those so treated. ³⁴You even joined in the sufferings of those in prison and joyfully accepted the confiscation of your property, knowing that you had a better and lasting possession. ³⁵Therefore, do not throw away your confidence; it will have great recompense.(³⁶You need endurance to do the will of God and receive what he has promised.)

³⁷"For, after just a brief moment,
 he who is to come shall come;
 he shall not delay.
³⁸But my just one shall live by faith,
 and if he draws back I take no
 pleasure in him."

³⁹We are not among those who draw back and perish, but among those who have faith and will possess life.

10:22-25 feature the virtues of faith, hope, and love. The call to approach God in faith ("with a sincere heart and in absolute trust") in 10:22 builds upon the conviction that Christ's perfect sacrifice has brought about the forgiveness of sins—an experience that is symbolized in baptism. The call to persevere in Christian hope in 10:23 builds on the trustworthiness of God and of God's promises. The call to live in love with fellow Christians in 10:24-25 builds upon the need for Christian community to be the place where Christians encourage one another to love and to do good works in preparation for the Day of the Lord (judgment). The passing observation that some were absenting themselves from the Christian assembly (10:25) is another symptom of the ecclesial situation of the community to which the author wrote.

The stern warning in 10:26-31 (see 6:4-8) again concerns a post-baptismal sin of the most serious kind—apostasy (see 10:29). If one rejects Christ after having embraced Christian faith, there is no effective sacrifice for one's sins because the sacrifices of the old covenant have been superseded and the all-sufficient sacrifice of Christ has been rejected. All that remains for such persons is the "fearful prospect" of judgment and punishment. The seriousness of their sin is highlighted by another argument "from the lesser to the greater." If according to Deuteronomy 17:6 a person may be

V. Examples, Discipline, Disobedience

11 Faith of the Ancients. [1]Faith is the realization of what is hoped for and evidence of things not seen. [2]Because of it the ancients were well attested. [3]By faith we understand that the universe was ordered by the word of God, so that what is visible came into being through the invisible. [4]By faith Abel offered to God a sacrifice greater than Cain's. Through this he was attested to be righteous, God bearing witness to his gifts, and through this, though dead, he still speaks. [5]By faith Enoch was taken up so that he should not see death, and "he was found no

---

put to death for idolatry or blasphemy on the testimony of two or three human witnesses, how much greater will the punishment be for those who spurn the Son of God, profane the blood of God's covenant, and commit outrages against the holy Spirit. The fearsome character of God's judgment is reinforced by quotations from Deuteronomy 32:35-36: "Vengeance is mine; I will repay . . . The Lord will judge his people." This stern warning concludes with one of the most menacing sentences in Scripture: "It is a fearful thing to fall into the hands of the living God" (10:31).

As in 6:9-12, the stern warning is balanced by a word of hope and encouragement in 10:32-39. The author in 10:32-34 urges the community to recall what they suffered shortly after having become Christians ("after you had been enlightened"). The way in which these sufferings are described—public abuse, imprisonment, and confiscation of property—may reflect conditions that prevailed at Rome for some Christians in the late fifties or early sixties of the first century A.D. The preacher's point is that the new Christians endured these sufferings joyfully because they were convinced that they had "a better and lasting possession" (10:34). He goes on in 10:35-36 to exhort these people to confidence and endurance in the present situation out of the conviction that they will surely be rewarded by God ("great recompense . . . receive what he has promised"). Then in 10:37-38 he appeals to the second coming of Christ with a christological interpretation of Isaiah 26:20 ("he who is to come shall come") and urges perseverance in faith by quoting Habakkuk 2:4 ("my just one shall live by faith"). He ends in 10:39 by counting himself and his community "among those who have faith and will possess life," thus preparing for the catalogue of biblical exemplars of faith in chapter 11.

11:1-40 Examples of persevering faith

To explain what it means to be "among those who have faith and will possess life" (10:39), the author presents a catalogue of figures from the Old Testament who provide models of persevering faith in God's promises.

more because God had taken him." Before he was taken up, he was attested to have pleased God. [6]But without faith it is impossible to please him, for anyone who approaches God must believe that he exists and that he rewards those who seek him. [7]By faith Noah, warned about what was not yet seen, with reverence built an ark for the salvation of his household. Through this he condemned the world and inherited the righteousness that comes through faith.

[8]By faith Abraham obeyed when he was called to go out to a place that he was to receive as an inheritance; he went out, not knowing where he was to go. [9]By faith he sojourned in the promised land as in a foreign country, dwelling in tents with Isaac and Jacob, heirs of the same promise; [10]for he was looking forward to the city with foundations, whose architect and maker is God. [11]By faith he received power to generate, even though he was past the normal age—and Sarah herself was sterile—for he thought that the one who had made the promise was trustworthy. [12]So it was that there came forth from one man, himself as good as dead, descendants as numerous as the stars in the sky and as countless as the sands on the seashore.

[13]All these died in faith. They did not receive what had been promised but saw it and greeted it from afar and acknowledged themselves to be strangers and aliens on earth, [14]for those who speak thus show that they are seeking a homeland. [15]If they had been thinking of the land from which they had come, they would have had opportunity to return. [16]But now they

---

Similar lists of biblical heroes can be found in Sirach 44–49 and Wisdom 10:1–11:4. What distinguishes the list in Hebrews 11 is the resolute emphasis on "by faith." For the author of Hebrews, faith involves the knowledge of unseen realities, a generous response to God's call, a hopeful trust in God's promises, and faithful endurance in the face of suffering and death.

What may appear to be an abstract definition of faith in 11:1-2 is more a programmatic statement to be illustrated by the examples that follow. That faith involves trust in God's promises ("what is hoped for . . . things not seen") is clear. The problem comes with the Greek words *hypostasis* ("realization") and *elenchos* ("evidence"), and whether they are to be taken as objectively as those translations suggest or in a more subjective way ("assurance . . . conviction"). Of course, faith involves both objective and subjective dimensions, as the following examples will show.

The first examples (11:3-7) correspond to events and figures in Genesis 1–11. The work of creation described in Genesis 1 (11:3) was carried out by the power of God's word, and we understand this to be so "by faith." The reason why God accepted the sacrifice of Abel rather than that of Cain (see Gen 4:1-7) is attributed in 11:4 to Abel's superior faith and righteousness. The reason why Enoch was taken up into heaven (see Gen 5:24) was his

desire a better homeland, a heavenly one. Therefore, God is not ashamed to be called their God, for he has prepared a city for them.

◄ ¹⁷By faith Abraham, when put to the test, offered up Isaac, and he who had received the promises was ready to offer his only son, ¹⁸of whom it was said, "Through Isaac descendants shall

◄ bear your name." ¹⁹He reasoned that God was able to raise even from the dead, and he received Isaac back as a symbol. ²⁰By faith regarding things still to come Isaac blessed Jacob and Esau. ²¹By faith Jacob, when dying, blessed each of the sons of Joseph and "bowed

in worship, leaning on the top of his staff." ²²By faith Joseph, near the end of his life, spoke of the Exodus of the Israelites and gave instructions about his bones.

²³By faith Moses was hidden by his parents for three months after his birth, because they saw that he was a beautiful child, and they were not afraid of the king's edict. ²⁴By faith Moses, when he had grown up, refused to be known as the son of Pharaoh's daughter; ²⁵he chose to be ill-treated along with the people of God rather than enjoy the fleeting pleasure of sin. ²⁶He considered the reproach of the Anointed greater

---

great faith, according to 11:5. The case of Enoch leads to a brief reflection in 11:6 on the life of faith as the only life that is pleasing to God and on the necessity for belief in God and in God's desire to reward those who seek him. In the cases of creation, Abel's sacrifice, and Enoch's assumption, the author has provided an interpretation ("by faith") that is not explicit in the biblical texts. In the case of Noah (11:7) he has a strong biblical example of faith. According to Genesis 6:8-22, Noah obeyed God's command to build an ark on the strength of his trust in God's promises "about what was not yet seen" and he was rewarded by "the salvation of his household." Noah's act of faith was both a witness against the corrupt world and a foreshadowing of Abraham's "righteousness that comes through faith."

A second set of biblical examples of faith is provided by Abraham and other patriarchs in 11:8-22. According to 11:8-10, faith is what motivated Abraham to leave his homeland and to enter the promised land of Canaan (see Gen 12:1-4), even though he did not know where he was going. And yet by "dwelling in tents" he acknowledged that the promised land of Canaan was not to be his perfect and final abode. Rather, it was a sign or shadow of the heavenly city of God, "the city with foundations, whose architect and maker is God." Faith, according to 11:11-12, is what enabled Abraham and Sarah to accept the promise (see Gen 17:15-22) that despite their advanced ages and her sterility they would have a son named Isaac, and that their descendants would be as many as "the stars in the sky" and "the sands on the seashore." Abraham's faith rested on the person of God: "for he thought that the one who made the promise was trustworthy" (11:11).

49

wealth than the treasures of Egypt, for he was looking to the recompense. [27]By faith he left Egypt, not fearing the king's fury, for he persevered as if seeing the one who is invisible. [28]By faith he kept the Passover and sprinkled the blood, that the Destroyer of the first-born might not touch them. [29]By faith they crossed the Red Sea as if it were dry land, but when the Egyptians attempted it they were drowned. [30]By faith the walls of Jericho fell after being encircled for seven days. [31]By faith Rahab the harlot did not perish with the disobedient, for she had received the spies in peace.

[32]What more shall I say? I have not time to tell of Gideon, Barak, Samson, Jephthah, of David and Samuel and the prophets, [33]who by faith conquered kingdoms, did what was righteous, obtained the promises; they closed the mouths of lions, [34]put out raging fires, escaped the devouring sword; out of weakness they were made powerful, became strong in battle, and turned back foreign invaders. [35]Women received back their dead through resurrection. Some were tortured and would not accept deliverance, in order to obtain a better resurrection. [36]Others endured mockery, scourging, even chains and imprisonment. [37]They were stoned, sawed in two, put to death at sword's point; they went about in skins of sheep or goats, needy, afflicted, tormented. [38]The world was not worthy of them. They wandered about in deserts and on mountains, in caves and in crevices in the earth.

In 11:13-16 the author interrupts his list for a reflection on the as-yet-unfulfilled or eschatological nature of the faith displayed by Abraham and Sarah and indeed by all the great Old Testament exemplars of faith. Since "all these died in faith," they failed to enjoy during their lifetimes on earth the fullness of life with God—something that has been made possible through Jesus' death, resurrection, and exaltation. Rather, they remained "strangers and aliens on earth" (11:14; see Gen 23:4) in search of a homeland. However, they recognized that their true homeland was not the land from which they came (and to which they could return) but rather the city that God had prepared for them in heaven. What these heroes of faith hoped for has become a reality through Christ.

The theme of the as-yet-unfulfilled character of the patriarchs' faith is developed by further examples in 11:17-22. Faith moved Abraham to offer his son Isaac as a sacrifice to God, despite the fact that God's promise of many descendants was to be through Isaac (11:17-19). What made Abraham willing to obey God's command was, according to the author, a belief in God's power to raise the dead back to life, and so Isaac was a symbol foreshadowing the resurrection of Jesus. The blessings bestowed by Isaac and Jacob (11:20-21) were signs of their hopes for future generations. The observation that Jacob gave his blessing while "leaning on the top of his

³⁹Yet all these, though approved because of their faith, did not receive what had been promised. ⁴⁰God had foreseen something better for us, so that without us they should not be made perfect.

12 God Our Father. ¹Therefore, since we are surrounded by so

staff" (see Gen 47:31 in the Greek version) adds to the "pilgrim" motif of faith. The fact that Joseph gave instructions about the Exodus from Egypt and about moving his bones out of Egypt (11:22; see Gen 50:24-25) indicates the incomplete nature of what he experienced and his trust that there would be much more to the promises of God.

The faith displayed by the patriarchs was also at work in Moses and the Exodus generation according to 11:23-31. Faith led Moses' parents to conceal him in defiance of Pharaoh's decree to kill the male infants of the Hebrews (11:23; see Exod 2:1-10). Faith led Moses to identify himself not with the royal household of Egypt but rather with Israel as the people of God (11:24-27; see Exod 2:11-15), even though this meant suffering "the reproach of the Anointed" and so prefiguring the sufferings of Christ. Faith led Moses to command the elders of Israel in Egypt to sprinkle blood from the Passover lambs at the doors of the residences of the Hebrews (11:28; see Exod 12:21-23). He had no guarantee beyond his faith in God's promises that this action would protect the Israelites from "the Destroyer of the firstborn." Faith led Moses and others to cross the Red Sea with the conviction that they would emerge safely and that the Egyptians would not do so (11:29; see Exod 14:22-28). Faith led Joshua to trust that the walls of Jericho would fall (11:30; see Josh 6:12-21), and faith led the Gentile prostitute Rahab to ally herself with the people of God by protecting the Israelite spies (11:31; see Josh 2:1-21; 6:22-25).

A good preacher knows when to bring a topic to its conclusion ("What more shall I say?"), and so in 11:32-38 he summarizes the subsequent history of God's people. After a list of heroes (11:32), he gives examples of triumphant faith in 11:33-35a and still more examples of endurance in the face of suffering in 11:35b-38. These heroes bore their sufferings out of faith in the resurrection (see 11:35a), which was appropriate since this world "was not worthy of them" (11:38a).

However great was the faith that these heroes displayed, they nonetheless did not yet receive what had been promised (11:39-40). What God promised was forgiveness of sins and eternal life with God—something made possible through Jesus' death, resurrection, and exaltation. By contrasting the heroes of Old Testament faith and "us" (Christians), the

great a cloud of witnesses, let us rid ourselves of every burden and sin that clings to us and persevere in running the race that lies before us ²while keeping our eyes fixed on Jesus, the leader and perfecter of faith. For the sake of the joy that lay before him he endured the cross, despising its shame, and has taken his seat at the right of the throne of God. ³Consider how he endured such opposition from sinners, in order that you may not grow weary and lose heart. ⁴In your struggle against sin you have not yet resisted to the point of shedding blood. ⁵You have also forgotten the exhortation addressed to you as sons:

> "My son, do not disdain the discipline of the Lord
> or lose heart when reproved by him;
> ⁶for whom the Lord loves, he disciplines;
> he scourges every son he acknowledges."

⁷Endure your trials as "discipline"; God treats you as sons. For what "son" is there whom his father does not discipline? ⁸If you are without discipline, in which all have shared, you are not sons

---

author suggests that "we" have received what God promised and so are in a superior position to them.

12:1-17 A call to persevere in faith

The heroes of faith celebrated in chapter 11 constitute a "cloud of witnesses" for Christians (12:1). Nevertheless, the Christians addressed in this sermon are still engaged in a struggle or race that demands endurance and discipline. In this contest they have the good example of Jesus as "the leader and perfecter of faith" (12:2). What is especially significant for them is Jesus' own willingness to endure the suffering and shame of the cross in full expectation of his exaltation to God's throne (see Ps 110:1) and the perfect joy of life in heavenly glory. For Jesus, the cross was a trial to be endured in the hope of glory.

In 12:3-4 the preacher addresses the community's own situation in the light of Christ's example. His endurance of hostility from sinners should inspire them to "not grow weary and lose heart" (12:3). Moreover, their situation, however serious it may seem, in fact has not yet reached the point of "shedding blood" (12:4), which suggests that they have not yet faced martyrdom.

To help the community to understand its present sufferings and to encourage them to persevere in faith, the author offers a reflection on the theme of suffering as a discipline, with Proverbs 3:11-12 as his main text. His emphasis is on the educative or formative (rather than punitive) value of suffering. In the biblical passage quoted in 12:5-6 the sage directs his student ("my son") to accept the divine discipline as a sign of God's love

but bastards. [9]Besides this, we have had our earthly fathers to discipline us, and we respected them. Should we not [then] submit all the more to the Father of spirits and live? [10]They disciplined us for a short time as seemed right to them, but he does so for our benefit, in order that we may share his holiness. ([11]At the time, all discipline seems a cause not for joy but for pain, yet later it brings the peaceful fruit of righteousness to those who are trained by it.)

[12]So strengthen your drooping hands and your weak knees. [13]Make straight paths for your feet, that what is lame may not be dislocated but healed.

Penalties of Disobedience [14]Strive for peace with everyone, and for that holiness without which no one will see the Lord. [15]See to it that no one be deprived of the grace of God, that no bitter root spring up and cause trouble, through which many may become defiled, [16]that no one be an immoral or profane person like Esau, who sold his birthright for a single meal. [17]For you know that later, when he wanted to inherit his father's blessing, he was re-

---

and concern for him. In the biblical world a father had the ultimate responsibility for child rearing (especially in the case of sons). In his first application in 12:7-8 the preacher suggests that their present sufferings are proof that God regards the Christians as legitimate "sons" for whom he takes responsibility.

He goes on in 12:9-11 to compare the discipline applied by earthly fathers with the discipline applied by God. If earthly fathers win respect from the sons whom they discipline, how much more should we respect "the Father of spirits" in our sufferings (12:9). Moreover, the benefits from divine discipline—sharing in God's holiness, and "the peaceful fruit of righteousness"—in the present and the future far outweigh the benefits that may come from a human father's application of discipline. Divine discipline is superior to human discipline in forming children of God.

Rather than obsessing over their present sufferings, the addressees need to get back on the "way" of discipleship. Using language from Isaiah 35:3 and Proverbs 4:26, the preacher in 12:12-13 urges them to pull themselves together and walk along the straight path with renewed spiritual energy. They also need to remove whatever hinders their spiritual progress. Therefore, according to 12:14, they need to strive for the peace and holiness that come from God and that bears witness to God in the world. They need to guard against the "bitter root" (see Deut 29:18) of division that can harm the life of the whole community (12:15). And they need to learn from the negative example of Esau who because of his impatience and desire for momentary gratification (see Gen 25:29-34) sold his birthright to Jacob and could not get it back when he sought Isaac's

jected because he found no opportunity to change his mind, even though he sought the blessing with tears.

[18]You have not approached that which could be touched and a blazing fire and gloomy darkness and storm [19]and a trumpet blast and a voice speaking words such that those who heard begged that no message be further addressed to them, [20]for they could not bear to hear the command: "If even an animal touches the mountain, it shall be stoned." [21]Indeed, so fearful was the spectacle that Moses said, "I am terrified and trembling." [22]No, you have approached Mount Zion and the city of the living God, the heavenly Jerusalem, and countless angels in festal gathering, [23]and the assembly of the firstborn enrolled in heaven, and God the judge of all, and the spirits of the just made perfect, [24]and Jesus, the mediator of a new covenant, and the sprinkled blood that speaks more eloquently than that of Abel.

[25]See that you do not reject the one who speaks. For if they did not escape when they refused the one who warned them on earth, how much more in our case if we turn away from the one who warns from heaven! [26]His voice shook the earth at that time, but now he has promised, "I will once more shake not only earth but heaven." [27]That phrase, "once more," points to [the] removal of shaken, created things, so that what is unshaken may remain. [28]Therefore, we who are receiving the unshakable kingdom should have gratitude, with which we should offer worship pleasing to God in reverence and awe. [29]For our God is a consuming fire.

---

blessing (see Gen 27:30-45). The case of Esau reiterates in a subtle way the author's previous stern warnings about the impossibility of repentance after apostasy (see 6:4-8 and 10:26-31).

12:18-29 A call to heavenly worship

Through Christ's priestly sacrifice on the cross, we have access to God. What the institutions and rituals of the old covenant were powerless to do, Christ has accomplished by making possible right relationship with God (justification) and participation in the heavenly worship of God.

This point is developed in 12:18-24 by contrasting the old worship symbolized by Mount Sinai (12:18-21) and the new worship symbolized by Mount Zion (12:22-24). The description of Mount Sinai is taken mainly from Exodus 19 (see also Exod 20:18-21 and Deut 4:10), though what appears to be awesome in Exodus 19 is interpreted negatively as terrifying in Hebrews. The Sinai experience was full of violent images of storms, fire, and trumpet blasts. It featured a command (Exod 19:12-13) to stone any animal that touched the sacred mountain. Even Moses the mediator of the Sinai covenant confessed that he was "terrified and trembling" (Deut 9:19). By contrast, the new heavenly worship symbolized by Mount

VI. Final Exhortation, Blessing, Greetings

13 ¹Let mutual love continue. ²Do not neglect hospitality, for through it some have unknowingly entertained angels. ³Be mindful of prisoners as if sharing their imprisonment, and of the ill-treated as of yourselves, for you also are in the body. ⁴Let marriage be honored among all and the marriage bed be kept undefiled, for God will judge the immoral and adulterers. ⁵Let your life be free from love of money but be content with what you

---

Zion is peaceful and joyful. Here Mount Zion is not the earthly city of Jerusalem but rather the heavenly Jerusalem (see Revelation 21–22), "the city of the living God." It is inhabited by angels, "the firstborn enrolled in heaven" (perhaps the saints of the Old Testament, Christian martyrs, or Christians who had already died), God the judge of all, and Jesus the mediator of a new covenant. Whereas Abel's blood bore witness against Cain's guilt and cried out for vengeance (see Gen 4:10), Jesus' blood spoke more eloquently in that it won forgiveness of sins and brought about perfect reconciliation with God.

The contrast is followed by an admonition not to reject God's warning (12:25-29). In the new covenant of Mount Zion/heavenly Jerusalem it is God who speaks. If the people of the Sinai covenant refused to listen to Moses and were punished for their obduracy, how much more punishment can Christians expect if they fail to heed the heavenly voice of God and his Son (see 6:4-8; 10:26-31; 12:15-17).

While the author of Hebrews is generally concerned with realized eschatology (the present benefits of Christ's saving action) and spatial eschatology (heaven and earth), he does occasionally engage in temporal eschatology (as in 10:27-28). Here in 12:26-28 his biblical text is from Haggai 2:6: "I will once more shake not only earth but heaven." The earth shook at the giving of the old covenant at Mount Sinai (see Exod 19:18). But the sixth-century prophet Haggai spoke of a future shaking that would involve both earth and heaven. At God's future eschatological intervention both earth and heaven will shake. Nevertheless, the final shaking will be good news for those who have persevered in faith and in the worship of God. The result will be the removal of "shaken, created things" (12:27). Then the kingdom of God will be "the unshakable kingdom" in which the worship of God will be conducted "in reverence and awe." To those consoling and encouraging words, the preacher adds a concluding comment designed to bring his audience back to the serious challenge that faced them in the present: "For our God is a consuming fire" (12:29; see Deut 4:24; Isa 33:14).

have, for he has said, "I will never forsake you or abandon you." ⁶Thus we may say with confidence:

> "The Lord is my helper,
> [and] I will not be afraid.
> What can anyone do to me?"

⁷Remember your leaders who spoke the word of God to you. Consider the outcome of their way of life and imitate their faith.(⁸Jesus Christ is the same yesterday, today, and forever.)

⁹Do not be carried away by all kinds of strange teaching. It is good to have our hearts strengthened by grace and not by foods, which do not benefit those who live by them. ¹⁰We have an altar from which those who serve the tabernacle have no right to eat. ¹¹The bodies of the animals whose blood the high priest brings into the sanctuary as a sin offering are burned outside the camp. ¹²Therefore, Jesus also suffered outside the gate, to consecrate the people by his own blood.(¹³Let us then go to him outside the camp, bearing the reproach that he bore.)¹⁴For here we have no lasting city, but we seek the one that is to come. ¹⁵Through him [then] let us continually offer God a sacrifice of praise, that is, the fruit of

---

13:1-6 General instructions

Under the heading "let mutual love continue" (13:1), the author encourages the cultivation of the human virtues of hospitality, compassion, chastity, and avoidance of greed. In each case he provides a theological motivation.

As Acts and the New Testament epistles show, there was an extensive network of communication among early Christians. The virtue of hospitality toward emissaries (apostles) and other travelers was essential to its smooth functioning. The theological motive about receiving angels attached to the admonition not to neglect hospitality (13:2) alludes to episodes involving Abraham and Lot in Genesis 18 and 19. The directive to be mindful of prisoners and victims of torture (13:3) is accompanied by an appeal to human solidarity. The call to respect marriage and to avoid adultery (13:4) invokes God's judgment against fornicators and adulterers (see 1 Cor 5:13; Eph 5:5). The rejection of greed (13:5) is balanced by contentment with what God gives. The theological motive for such an attitude is trust in God as expressed in God's own promise according to Deuteronomy 31:6, 8. The concluding confession in 13:6 quotes Psalm 118(117):6 to the effect that confidence in God casts out all fear. In this short instruction the motives are quite varied: biblical precedents, human solidarity, divine judgment, and trust in God. The absence of a direct appeal to Christ in these instructions is unusual in a work that is so directly centered on Christ as Hebrews is.

Ruins of a temple near Miletus in modern Turkey

lips that confess his name. (¹⁶Do not neglect to do good and to share what you
have; God is pleased by sacrifices of
that kind.

¹⁷Obey your leaders and defer to
them, for they keep watch over you

and will have to give an account, that
they may fulfill their task with joy and
not with sorrow, for that would be of
no advantage to you.

¹⁸Pray for us, for we are confident
that we have a clear conscience, wish-

13:7-17 Community life and worship

This section begins and ends with instructions about "leaders" (13:7-9
and 13:17), and contains an intervening reflection on worship (13:10-16).
The leaders "who spoke the word of God to you" may include not only
those who actually evangelized the group addressed in this work but also
the apostles and even the Old Testament heroes of faith celebrated in chapter 11. The statement in 13:8 that "Jesus Christ is the same yesterday, today,
and forever" sounds like an early Christian confession of faith, and at the
same time fits well with the emphasis in Hebrews on Christ as the eternal
leader of God's people. This confession is followed by a warning in 13:9
not to be swayed by "strange teaching." The example of "foods, which do
not benefit those who live by them" may refer to the Old Testament sacrifices or to the Jewish food laws. If, however, Hebrews was directed to a
Jewish Christian community at Rome (as many scholars think likely), then
there may be an allusion to the struggle between the "weak" and the
"strong" treated by Paul in Romans 14–15. The author of Hebrews clearly
takes the side of the "strong."

The intervening section on worship (13:10-16) begins in 13:10 by making a distinction in the worship of the old covenant and the new covenant.
The "altar" refers more likely to the heavenly sanctuary at which Christ
the high priest presides than to a church building or even to community
celebrations of the Eucharist. Those who continue to "serve the tabernacle" (under the old covenant) have no right to the "altar" of Christ (under
the new covenant). If (as seems likely) the original addressees were Jewish
Christians, this statement expresses a sharp distinction between "old covenant" Judaism and "new covenant" Jewish Christianity.

In 13:11-12 the author makes a final attempt to explain Jesus' death in
terms of sacrifice. According to Leviticus 16:27, the carcasses of the animals whose blood was used in the Day of Atonement ritual were to be
taken outside the camp and burned. In Jesus' time it was forbidden to
hold an execution within the city walls of the holy city of Jerusalem.
Therefore Jesus was crucified at Golgotha, a small hill which was outside

ing to act rightly in every respect. ¹⁹I especially ask for your prayers that I may be restored to you very soon. ²⁰May the God of peace, who brought up from the dead the great shepherd of the sheep by the blood of the eternal covenant, Jesus our Lord, ²¹furnish you with all that is good, that you may do his will. May he carry out in you what is pleasing to him through Jesus Christ, to whom be glory forever [and ever]. Amen. ²²Brothers, I ask you to bear with this message of encouragement, for I

---

the city walls. Thus according to 13:12 Jesus suffered "outside the gate" in accord with the type or pattern laid out in Leviticus 16. His death was the perfect atoning sacrifice. In light of this typology, the author invites the community to "go to him outside the camp" (13:13) and thus share in the shame that Jesus suffered in his crucifixion. Such action will confirm that their true city is the heavenly Jerusalem ("the one that is to come") and that they have "no lasting city" on earth.

What is true worship for these Jewish Christians? It is not to be found in the sacrifices of the old covenant. Rather, according to 13:15-16, Christian worship is preeminently the praise of God and good deeds. Only here does the author "spiritualize" the concept of sacrifice and relate it to acts of public worship ("a sacrifice of praise") and to good works done by Christians ("God is pleased by sacrifices of that kind," 13:16). Elsewhere, the focus has been on the material sacrifices of the old covenant and the death of Christ interpreted as the perfect sacrifice of the new covenant. The extent to which the "sacrifice of praise" might refer to the Eucharist remains uncertain.

The section ends in 13:17 by returning to the topic of "leaders." Here the leaders are clearly those who presently exercise oversight in the Christian community addressed in this work. The author urges respect for and cooperation with these leaders as being most beneficial for both the leaders and the community.

13:18-25 Final prayers and greetings

The author first in 13:18-19 requests prayers on his own behalf. He attests to the purity of his own intentions ("we have a clear conscience") and hopes to meet soon with the community in person. He clearly knows these people personally, and may well count himself among their leaders (see 13:17).

Then in 13:20-21 the author formulates a prayer on behalf of the community. He prays first (13:20-21a) that God may enable them to do God's will, and then (13:21b) he asks that God may carry out in them what is

have written to you rather briefly. [23]I must let you know that our brother Timothy has been set free. If he comes soon, I shall see you together with him. [24]Greetings to all your leaders and to all the holy ones. Those from Italy send you greetings. [25]Grace be with all of you.

---

pleasing to God. God is the beginning and the end of all their good works. The description of Jesus as "the great shepherd of the sheep" is unique in Hebrews (but see John 10:11 and 1 Pet 5:4), whereas the reference to Jesus' resurrection and to "the blood of the eternal covenant" are prominent themes throughout the work.

The request for a favorable reception in 13:22 consists of what is generally regarded as the author's own description of his sermon in written form ("this message of encouragement") and a somewhat disingenuous comment about his having written "rather briefly." The personal information in 13:23 provides a reference to Timothy that is the work's only real link to Paul. Assuming that this is Paul's co-worker, we may suppose that the author knew Timothy. Or perhaps the reference to Timothy was interpolated later to make a connection with Paul and his circle.

The greeting in 13:24a is directed to both the "leaders" (see 13:7, 17) and "all the holy ones" (a common way of referring to Christians). Many scholars find in 13:24b ("those from Italy send you greetings") grounds for supposing that the recipients are in Italy (most likely in Rome), and that the author is conveying greetings from Italians who are living where he is (outside Italy). The text, however, is ambiguous, and it could be read in the opposite way to indicate that the sermon in written form was sent from Italy to another place outside Italy.

The final blessing in 13:25 ("grace be with all of you") is both formulaic (see Titus 3:15) and at the same time expressive of the author's theology of Christ's priestly sacrifice as the ultimate and effective manifestation of God's favor toward humankind.

REVIEW AIDS AND DISCUSSION TOPICS

1:1–4:13 God's Son and God's Word *(pages 11–23)*

1. From the prologue in Hebrews 1:1-4 what themes can you expect the author to develop in the body of the work?

2. How would you describe the author's approach to the Old Testament on the basis of Hebrews 1:5-14 and 2:5-9? What are the presuppositions? What is the logic on which the scriptural arguments are based?

3. What positive teachings about Christian life and community does the author draw from the negative example of the Exodus generation in the wilderness according to Psalm 95?

4. What constitutes the "rest" that the author wants Christians to seek? How does he use biblical texts to develop that understanding?

5. In what sense is the word of God (Scripture) a "two-edged sword"? Have you ever experienced Scripture to be such in your life?

4:14–10:18 The Priesthood and Sacrifice of Christ *(pages 23–44)*

1. On what grounds does the author establish in 4:14–5:10 the high priesthood of Christ?

2. What is the nature of the sin warned against in Hebrews 6:4-8 (see also 10:26-31)? What makes this sin so serious?

3. What features in the Day of Atonement ritual described in Leviticus 16 does the author use to develop his portrait of Christ the high priest?

4. What elements in the biblical texts about Melchizedek (Gen 14:17-20 and Ps 110:4) contribute to the case for the priesthood of Christ? Do you find the argument convincing?

5. Has God's covenant with Israel been revoked? Compare the approach in Hebrews to Paul's meditation in Romans 9–11. Do they agree?

6. People in biblical times understood sacrifice in terms of a gift to God, communion with God, and expiation for sins. How do these elements contribute to the understanding of Christ's death as a sacrifice in Hebrews?

7. What did blood symbolize for the author of Hebrews? What does it symbolize for you?

10:19–13:25 Perseverance in Christian Life *(pages 44–60)*

1. What sufferings had the community addressed in Hebrews undergone? How does the author expect that their belief in Christ will help them to persevere in the midst of their sufferings?

2. On the basis of the examples of biblical faith in Hebrews 11, what characteristics of faith seem to be most important? How do they correspond to your own faith experience?

3. How do you react to the understanding of suffering as divine discipline presented in 12:1-17?

4. What picture of Christian worship emerges from 12:18-29 and 13:7-17?

General Topics

1. What elements in Hebrews do you find most helpful or appealing? What is most difficult or problematic?

2. In what respects does Hebrews agree with other New Testament books? Where does it differ? What special theological significance does it have within the New Testament taken as a whole?

3. Do you see parallels between the Christ of Hebrews and the Jesus of the Gospels?

4. How are Christ's sufferings related to our sufferings and to our salvation in the light of Hebrews?

5. How does the author balance the humanity and the divinity of Jesus?

6. How might Hebrews speak to your Christian community today? Do you find similar problems? How might an appeal to Christ's sacrifice and priesthood provide guidance?

7. What significance might the priesthood of Christ have for Christian life and ministry today?

8. Is it fair to call Hebrews anti-Jewish? What elements might support such a judgment? What might speak against it?

9. How has your study of Hebrews contributed to your understanding of Christian preaching? In the light of Hebrews what constitutes a good sermon?

INDEX OF CITATIONS FROM THE
CATECHISM OF THE CATHOLIC CHURCH

The arabic number(s) following the citation refer to the paragraph number(s) in the *Catechism of the Catholic Church*. The asterisk following a paragraph number indicates that the citation has been paraphrased.

Index of Citations from the Catechism of the Catholic Church

11:40	147	12:22-23	2188	13:15	1330
12:1-2	165	12:23	1021*	13:17	1269
12:1	1161, 2683*	13:3	2447*	13:20	632*
12:2	147	13:10	1182*		
12:3	569,* 598*	13:14	2796*		